NORTHAMPTO
Villages

Text by the Northamptonshire County Federation
of Women's Institutes
Photographs by Bill Meadows

COUNTRYSIDE BOOKS
Newbury, Berkshire

COUNTRYSIDE BOOKS
3 Catherine Road
Newbury, Berkshire

To view our complete range of books,
please visit us at
www.countrysidebooks.co.uk

ISBN 1 85306 764 4

The front cover photograph shows Hargrave,
the back cover photograph shows Nether Heyford village sign
and the picture on page 1 shows the view over Blisworth

Designed by Graham Whiteman

Typeset by Techniset Typesetters, Newton-le-Willows
Produced through MRM Associates Ltd., Reading
Printed in Italy

FOREWORD

When our WIs collaborated in the publishing of the original *Northamptonshire Village Book* in 1989, Caroline Raven, our then Chairman, wrote of the county's history, architecture, industrial heritage and the products of our fruitful land. She also mentioned the late twentieth century expansion of our towns that was well underway.

In recent years even more new industries and houses have grown up alongside the major transport routes that pass through our county. Despite this urbanisation and modernisation, Northamptonshire still has around 1,000 square miles of lovely Middle England countryside to enjoy.

We have notable churches of all periods; the gunpowder plotters were here; our ancestors witnessed one of the great battles of the civil war at Naseby; and, later, gangs of navvies built the canals and railways which were the wonders of their day and still in use. Great families of history lived and built their houses and estates here, and royalty stayed, passed through or, in the case of Mary Queen of Scots, died here. All through the years, the more ordinary people worked the land, raised stock, quarried iron ore, made iron and steel, tanned leather, manufactured boots and shoes and otherwise worked hard for a living. The evidence is here still and attracts many visitors.

Northamptonshire remains a county of high levels of employment and has easy access to all parts of the country. We who live here are blessed; there is plenty to delight us daily and we recommend our county to you, even if you can't stay long.

Malvina Keech
Federation Chairman
Northamptonshire County Federation of Women's Institutes
Autumn 2002

Aldwincle's attractive village sign

⌘ ALDWINCLE

Aldwincle, mentioned in the Domesday Book as Eldwincle, was probably so named from the Saxon word 'wincel', meaning bend or corner. The river Nene has a great double bend between Thorpe Waterville and Wadenhoe and it is here Aldwincle is situated.

Gathering to itself the calm and beauty of the valley, stands All Saints' church, now redundant. There is a brass to William Aldewynkle, dated 1463, in the chancel floor. Its 15th century tower has carved heads and figures, while its 13th century interior has fine proportions of space and arch, emphasised by the lack of furniture, making it a perfect setting for exhibitions, fund raising and plays.

The houses in Aldwincle are varied in style, with grey stone and red brick predominating. Here and there are handsomely thatched cottages; others are slated or pantiled. Many are graced with climbing roses, wisteria, clematis and forsythia.

Watching over it all is St Peter's church, dating from the 12th century and with many interesting features. It is reputed to have one of the best broach spires in the county, topped by a gleaming weathercock.

Twelve red may trees and most of the village seats were provided by the Spendlove family. Old villagers remember the 'Tommy loaf' and the coal charities. Twelve loaves for widows were baked in the bakehouse, which still exists as a building. The loaf and coal charities, because of shortages during the Second World War, were incorporated as money in the Green charity which exists today, giving money each year to those who apply and are considered suitable recipients. The money originally came from rent for land near the village but eventually the land was sold and the money invested to continue the charity for the 'poor, needy and thrifty'.

John Dryden, the poet and playwright, was born at the rectory opposite All Saints' church in 1631 and was christened there. Thomas Fuller, divine and historian, was born in the rectory of St Peter's in 1608. The rectory was pulled down circa 1790, but it stood in today's Rectory Field. When Fuller was curate at St Benet's, Cambridge he buried Thomas Hobson, the carrier, who used to hire out horses. Anyone hiring a horse could not choose their animal but had to have the horse nearest the stable door! The term 'Hobson's choice' exists today, meaning no choice at all!

⌘ APETHORPE

The village of Apethorpe, which lies on the road between King's Cliffe and Woodnewton, is mentioned in the Domesday Book, and the famous Hall was built by Sir Walter Mildmay in the 16th century, when he was lord of the manor. It is now in private ownership and is not open to the public, but the attractive facade can be seen from the road between Apethorpe and Woodnewton.

Cottages at Apethorpe

The village was originally all part of the manorial estate, and the names of houses such as Dairy Cottage, The Keeper's House, Laundry Cottage and The Old Post Office all give an idea of what would once have been found here. Some modern building has taken place, and conversion of old farm buildings into dwelling houses, but they are designed to blend with the old – of local stone, built at various times between the 16th century and the present day, with roofs of thatch or Collyweston slate.

The stream which flows through the village, the Willow Brook (called by locals 'The Willy Brook'), is a tributary of the river Nene, and passes under a picturesque hump-back bridge, flanked by thatched cottages which lead towards the church.

Opposite the church are the original stocks and whipping post once used to chastise offenders!

There is evidence of a church building dating back to the 12th century, but the present church of St Leonard celebrated its 500th anniversary in the 1980s. The Mildmay Chapel was added in 1621 as a memorial to Sir Anthony Mildmay and his wife, Lady Grace, whose effigies lie on the sarcophagus. The stained glass window in the chapel is of very fine workmanship.

Surrounded by arable farmland, this small village is a haven of peaceful, rural England.

⌘ ASHBY ST LEDGERS

The village is tucked into the north-western corner of the county, almost into Warwickshire. The Domesday Book entry gives the place name Ascebi (ash tree settlement). 'St Ledgers' is a corruption of the name of St Leodegarius, the patrol saint of the church, which stands at the east end of the village beside the manor house. Both buildings are of ancient foundation.

The manor was gifted to Hugh de Grentemaisnil by William the Conqueror and passed to various other occupants until about 1375 when it became the principal residence of the Catesby family and remained so for nearly 250 years. William Catesby was one of the favourites of Richard III. After the defeat of Richard by Henry Tudor at the Battle of Bosworth in 1485, William was beheaded. A Robert Catesby later became one of the leading figures in the Gunpowder Plot, and the half-timbered gatehouse next to the church is reputed to be the meeting place used by the conspirators.

There are memorials to the Catesbys in the church, along with several other fine brasses and monuments. During the Reformation, unfortunately, the wall paintings here were defaced and the rood destroyed, but the remaining rood screen is still magnificent and some of the wall paintings have now been uncovered. There is a rare Jacobean three-decker pulpit.

Early last century the manor became the property of Ivor Churchill Guest, 1st Viscount Wimborne, Lord Lieutenant of Ireland, who employed the architect Sir Edwin Lutyens to remodel some of the manor house, and to design the row of thatched cottages which stand on the north side of the main street.

After these historic events, the village now presents a very peaceful and attractive appearance, especially in springtime when the wide verges are flowery with daffodils, almond and cherry blossom.

⌘ ASHLEY

The village of Ashley is situated on the border with Leicestershire, and settlement here probably dates back to Roman times, since many relics were discovered not far from the village during the construction of the railway in the 19th century. Ashley station and the railway line were closed in the 1950s.

The church of St Mary the Virgin occupies a prominent position on the north side of the village and is built of warm brown ironstone and silver grey limestone. The interior is a resplendent blaze of colour since it was restored by the Rev Pulteney who paid for all the alterations himself, under the direction of the architect Gilbert Scott. Not only was he vicar from 1853 to 1874 but he was also the village squire and the stained glass window was dedicated to his memory. He also installed the organ in 1868 and built the village school (opposite the church) in 1858. This was used by local children until 1966.

The manor house situated to the north of the church, in Hall Lane, contains a room previously known as the Court Room, where the lord of the manor used to collect his dues at regular intervals during the year.

The Welland valley has always been mainly an agricultural area and it must have been thirsty work because at one time the village supported five inns!

Before the Second World War Ashley was a very different place from today. The beer for the George public house was brought up from the cellar in jugs and 'Devil among the tailors' and table skittles were popular games, with darts just being introduced. There was a village cricket team that was very well known in the district and bread and cakes were baked by the village baker. Milk, creamy and thick, came straight from the farm. All this now no longer exists. The local bus service was very good and the railway enabled villagers to be mobile, but most of the youngsters cycled or walked. They attended the surrounding village dances where all the families knew each other, having lived in the same villages for generations. The Fat Stock Show at Market Harborough was one of the highlights of the year.

⌘ AYNHO

Aynho has a recorded existence back to the time of Edward the Confessor, although the spelling of the name has changed over the centuries. Nearly all the buildings in the old part of the village are of local limestone and most were originally thatched. Many have been reroofed in slate or tile and, slates needing a less steep pitch than thatch, it can be seen how the walls were raised to create extra room inside. The oldest cottages in the village, formerly known as Pintle Row, are on Blacksmiths Hill. One has a 60 ft well in the front garden and dates from around 1500.

The Cartwright Arms, an old coaching inn, was named after the family who were the squires of the village from 1616 to the 1950s. The original manor house was burnt down during the Civil War by Royalist troops retreating from the battle of Naseby. Charles II paid the family compensation after his restoration to the throne and Park House was restored in 1680. A tragic car accident in 1954 killed the squire and his son, and the estate has now been broken up and is in private hands.

The church of St Michael and All Angels is built of limestone and the tower is 14th century. Severe damage was caused to the church during the Civil War and the main body was demolished in 1723, then rebuilt in the Grecian style. Outside is the old preaching cross.

From the churchyard can be seen the old icehouse in the grounds of Aynho Park, which was used to store ice in the days before refrigeration. Lumps of ice cut from the canal would keep for up to two years when packed with straw in its depths.

Aynho vilage

The village hall was built in 1920 from stones taken from the ruined plaguehouse in Pesthouse Wood. Plague victims were once isolated there and villagers would leave them food every day at the boundary fence. There are many other interesting buildings in the village, including the Jacobean grammar school and the almshouses built in 1822 with a bequest from John Baker, an Oxford glazier.

There are still some examples to be seen of the famous apricot trees, grown against the side of cottages. They were traditionally on high rootstocks to prevent children from picking the apricots. It is thought that the fruit was given to the Park House as part payment of the rent for the cottages.

⌘ BADBY & FAWSLEY

Badby and Fawsley are joined by woods and parkland and lie at the extreme end of the Cotswolds. They are situated four miles west of Weedon on the Daventry to Banbury road. Fawsley is renowned for its centuries-old connection with the Knightley family and Badby has been described as one of the prettiest villages in the county. Its 180 acre wood is well known for its bluebells but is even more notable for its carpets of wood anemones. The wood is now incorporated in the Park of Fawsley and is surrounded by rolling farmland, which has long been hunted over by the Pytchley and Grafton huntsmen. Both Fawsley and Badby have very distinctive medieval churches dedicated to the Virgin Mary.

St Mary's church at Badby

One of the county's famous earthworks is Arbury Hill, half a mile north-west of the village and the highest point in the county. Standing on a 24 acre site at the top of this hill is the remains of a probable Roman settlement, as well as a Saxon camp. Though only a bare 735 ft high it nevertheless has wonderful views of the surrounding countryside. On a clear day the Malvern Hills are visible.

Badby has a long and varied history, first being mentioned in AD 833. The Abbot of Evesham had oversight of the populace until the Dissolution of the Monasteries, after which the manor passed to Sir Edmund Knightley. Thereafter much of the employment in the village was connected with the estate in one form or another. There were various gatehouses on the perimeter of the estate, and one of these, known as the Arch, was occupied until 1890. It is on Long Roods by the cricket and football pitches.

The village is lucky to have a very good youth hostel which is a splendid base from which to discover the footpaths and walks in the area. The Knightley Way from Badby to Greens Norton starts right opposite the church and many ramblers come to enjoy the delights of the countryside.

⌘ BARNWELL

For a small village, Barnwell has a lot to offer. The oldest cottages are built of local stone, and many still have thatch or Collyweston roofs. Recent planning policy has tried to ensure that new houses blend with their surroundings, and the brook, with its wooden footbridges, that runs along the centre of the main street has attracted many painters and photographers. A colony of ducks inhabits the brook, and the mature lime trees along its banks are particularly lovely in autumn.

The manor house at the north end of the village used to be the country home of the Duke and Duchess of Gloucester. Within the gardens are the handsome ruins of a 13th century castle, built for Berengarius le Moine, and haunted, so some have claimed, by a monk brandishing a whip!

A pretty stone bridge opposite the side entrance to the manor leads to a beech-lined footpath to St Andrew's church, with its carefully tended graveyard. The church dates back to the late 13th century, and among the carved flowers and leaves that decorate the north doorway is a face with its tongue sticking out. This is a medieval 'Jack-in-the-green', relating to a May Day custom when young men camouflaged themselves in leaves before flirting with the girls.

The Reverend Nicholas Latham, who died in 1620, has an elaborate monument near the altar, and it was he who originally endowed the almshouses that are situated opposite the church. He also endowed the village's first school – now a private dwelling called Tudor House in the main street.

At the bottom of the hill past the church is the village green with its tall cluster of lime trees, and a stone bridge that leads over to the Montagu Arms. Part of the pub building dates back to the 18th century, and it is a properly traditional country inn.

A long time ago, Barnwell was divided into two parishes, St Andrew's and All Saints, and part of the church of All Saints, its chancel, stands on a rise beside the lower end of the main street. The rest of the church was demolished in 1825 after falling into a bad state of repair, but the chancel was saved because it housed the family vault of the Montagu family, the Earls of Sandwich. It is well used for occasional worship, and has a very peaceful graveyard, with a lovely view – especially at sunset – over the fields behind. Near the entrance is an ancient gravestone carved in the image of a monk, and it is this monk who is said to haunt the All Saints end of Barnwell.

⌘ BARTON SEAGRAVE

Barton Seagrave has a charm of its own. Retaining an old world village atmosphere, it still enjoys the benefits of the town of Kettering barely two miles away.

In the 14th century there was a castle at Barton Seagrave ruled over by Lord Segrave (spelled without the 'a'), and he is the subject of a popular local ghost story. Segrave fell violently in love with the beautiful Lady Isabel, daughter of Lord Latimer of Burton Latimer. Alas, Isabel was already betrothed to Hugh Neville. Segrave ranted and raged and at last captured Isabel and imprisoned her in the rat-infested dungeons beneath the castle, but she still refused his advances.

Hugh Neville and her brother rescued her one night and had reached the ford of the Ise, when they heard Segrave galloping after them. They fought mid-stream in a terrific thunderstorm and Neville was killed and both Isabel and her brother were drowned. Isabel haunted Segrave to his death. The beautiful Lady Isabel still skims like a filmy white swan over the river Ise.

Barton Hall is reputed to have been built from stones from the castle in the reign of Queen Elizabeth I. In 1665 the house was given as a wedding present by William Trumbell to his daughter on her marriage to John Bridges. Their son, Northamptonshire's famous historian, was born at the Hall in 1666 – his memorial is displayed inside the church.

The tithe barn next to the church was used for the storage of flax, crops, hops and saffron in the 17th century. It is a most attractive home. Mullion dressed stone was found in the rebuilding, possibly from the castle.

⌘ BLAKESLEY CUM WOODEND

Blakesley is a picturesque village, situated roughly midway between Northampton and Banbury, five miles west of Towcester. In Saxon times the settlement was surrounded by Whittlebury Forest, hence Woodend.

The Hall, which stood on the south (Woodend) side of the brook, was formerly a hospice of the Knights of St John of Jerusalem. The last lord of the manor was Mr C.W. Bartholomew (1875–1919) who during his residence was a generous

Church Street, Blakesley, looking towards St Mary's

benefactor to the village. After standing empty for several years the Hall was, sadly, demolished in 1857.

One of the many novel innovations brought to Blakesley by Mr Bartholomew was a 15" gauge railway. The track, which ran between the Hall and the main-line station was laid down in 1903. Two American steam locomotives were used to pull the train of open carriages and in 1909 a petrol-driven locomotive, built by the well-known Northampton firm of Bassett-Lowke, was added to the rolling stock and given the name *Blacolvesley*. In 1939/40 the whole outfit was taken to Yorkshire.

A grammar school for boys was endowed by William Foxley in 1669, but lost its grammar school status in 1850. In 1876 a girls' school was built and in 1912 the boys' school was enlarged to accommodate children of both sexes. In view of the generosity of the squire, as Mr Bartholomew was known locally, who made a considerable subscription to the cost of the new school, the deeds of the now redundant girls' school were made over to him, and he in turn presented the building to the village for use as a village hall.

In the early part of the last century the village supported a resident doctor, a village policeman, a builder, two wheelwright/undertakers, two blacksmiths, four public houses and an outdoor beerhouse. All that remains today is one public house, the Bartholomew Arms, previously known as the Red Lion. There were also three or four cobblers.

⌘ BLISWORTH

Blisworth (or Blidesworde as it was recorded in the Domesday Book) lies snugly on the old A43 between Towcester and Northampton, surrounded by open farmland.

It retains much of its historical charm with many of the thatched cottages dating back to the 16th century. One house, at the bottom of Courteenhall Road, has a room still known today as the 'Brethren Room', although it is now the main living room. On one of the walls is a fine example of an early wall painting, a panel approximately 4 ft by 2 ft depicting the words of Psalm 143. Many of the houses are built of Blisworth ironstone together with Northampton sandstone, and the variation of light and dark materials is an interesting feature throughout the village. Blisworth ironstone was the first to be quarried in the county.

Blisworth is in the centre of the county and could have developed into a much larger community. In the 17th century it became the main stop-over for coaches from Cheltenham and Stratford, and the Grafton Arms, which today is a private house, standing opposite the mill, was a well-known roadside inn. During the 18th century with the coming of the Grand Union Canal, Blisworth again was the most convenient place for the loading and unloading of boats from London, Midlands and the North. However, Blisworth Hill was an obstacle for the canal engineers and whilst a tunnel was constructed to take the canal through the hill, the Blisworth Hill Railway was built to carry boats' cargoes *over* the hill.

Canal life – the approach to Blisworth Tunnel

The railway was opened in 1800 and ran until 1805 when the tunnel was opened – a tremendous feat of engineering. The contractor who excavated it was Barnes of Banbury, a man who could neither read nor write and who carried all his calculations and estimates in his head! Blisworth Tunnel is today the longest navigable canal tunnel in the country (3,075 yds long) and it is a great challenge to today's holiday boaters, who of course use Blisworth as a convenient stopping point for shopping or for refreshment at one of the two pubs in the village.

⌘ BODDINGTON

The parish of Boddington is recorded in the Domesday Book as 'Botendon'. The medieval church is mainly 15th century but has examples of 13th century work and some interesting external features. Its churchyard is known for its 80 species of lichens including one county rarity. The church registers date from 1558, when the manor and estate came into the Spencer family, but much of the land had been sold when both Upper and Lower Boddington were enclosed 200 years later. A copy of the Enclosure Map of 1759, unfortunately for Upper Boddington only, has been found in the church.

Most of the parish is still the traditional 'patchwork' landscape. Hedgerows are therefore a significant feature, particularly in May when the cuckoos call and hawthorn is in blossom. The rarer midland thorn, a woodland species, grows in

Upper Boddington and its medieval church

many of the pre-enclosure hedges as do those other indicators of ancient hedges: hazel, dogwood and field maple.

The villages themselves hold much of interest, with many listed buildings, the oldest thought to date from the 15th century.

⌘ BRAYBROOKE

Braybrooke is a small village three miles to the west of Desborough and three miles south-east of Market Harborough. The main London railway passes through the parish, which is situated in a valley bisected by the river Jordan.

The village is surrounded by fertile agricultural land, over 300 acres of which is glebe land bequeathed in the early 19th century by Mrs Field, wife of the rector. In the late 18th century the main village industry was weaving, and the rush industry was also important. One small field is still called 'Osier Beds'. Rural weaving declined with the growth of the Northern mills.

The old heart of the village was the 13th century church, which was surrounded by cottages long since demolished. Their stones were removed to build other houses, and their cobbled pavements and streets are from time to time uncovered by ploughing. The church is in Early English style. Braybrooke's rare vamping horn, an ancient musical instrument once used in the church, is now on loan to the Market Harborough museum.

The main site of historical interest is where the old castle used to be. This was originally the manor of Robert de Braybrooke, which was rebuilt in the reign of King John. The castle was demolished about 1633 and a farmhouse was built on the site. This too fell into decay in the early part of the 20th century, and all that remains is the old farm brewhouse and a series of mounds marking the fishponds.

The village was subject to flooding in times of storms and melting snow, and in the 1980s a dam was built by Anglian Water across the river Jordan on the castle site to hold back surplus water and divert it into the fishponds.

The houses in the village are a mixture of old and new. The oldest date from the 16th century, with the Old Rectory and Bleak House being listed buildings along with the Latymers' stone bridge built in 1402.

⌘ BRIGSTOCK

Brigstock's origins go back to the Iron Age but the Brigstock we know today began as a Saxon settlement in a clearing in Rockingham Forest. The church shows much evidence of its Saxon origins and has one of the finest Saxon arches in Europe. Until comparatively recently the church bell was tolled three times a day to guide travellers lost in the woods between Brigstock and Weldon.

In the Middle Ages Brigstock developed into one of the largest villages in the Royal Forest and became a centre for administering the Forest Law. However, as early as the time of Elizabeth I the village had gained notoriety as the haunt of deer-stealers and by the time of Charles I it was common practice for villagers to defy the keepers and hunt at will.

The ill reputation the village acquired at this time was probably not helped by the high number of licensed premises which flourished in the 17th and 18th centuries. At least twelve buildings have been public houses at some time in their history.

Hunting has always been part of life in this area, wolves as well as foxes being hunted in the Middle Ages. In 1873 the Woodland Pytchley Hunt broke away from the North Pytchley Hunt and set up its kennels at Brigstock, where they remain. Lord Lonsdale came with his young wife to hunt from the Three Cocks and in 1881 took over the mastership. He kept 72 chestnut horses stabled in the village and brought with him one of the finest packs of hounds of the day. The Ring and its stabling at the junction of Kennel Hill and Stable Hill was built by the Duke of Buccleuch in 1873. In the 1980s the land was sold and a small development of houses built there.

To counteract the multiplicity of pubs, Brickstock entered early into the field of education. The first school was endowed in 1620 by the Rev Nicholas Latham, parson of Barnwell, near Oundle. He was the son of the keeper of Brigstock Great Park. The actual building no longer exists but it is the site of the war memorial on Hall Hill.

The obvious and actual centre of the village is Hall Hill, with its circle of stone houses around the ancient market cross, where since 1466 the village woman have sat and sold their produce. Edward IV granted a charter for a weekly market, but there were three days in the year when special markets or feasts were held.

There are many memories of Brigstock's more recent past told by our village elders. Between the two World Wars and for some years in the 1950s, Brigstock had a very good Silver Band. It also had a very small drummer and one day going down Church Street, the band turned right over the bridge towards Grafton, but the drummer, unable to see over the top of his drum, kept marching on to Thrapston!

⌘ THE BRINGTONS

The Bringtons, namely Great Brington, Little Brington and the hamlet of Nobottle are in the west of the county.

In the 19th century much of Brington, in common with the neighbouring villages of Harlestone and the Bramptons, became part of the Althorp Estate, home of the Spencers, and comparatively little land was in other ownership. It is interesting to compare the 1880s with today. In the 19th century the estate and its tenant farmers were the principal employers; the majority of the population dwelt under Estate roofs; the local blacksmith, whitesmith, shoemaker, tailor, carpenter, grocer and of course the licensed victualler provided for a self-sufficient community of over 800. Children were taught in schools established by successive Earls (by the 1880s the main school was being visited by Her Majesty's Inspectors) and by the turn of the century Reading Rooms for adults had been established in both villages. Early in the next decade piped water was taken to all properties and a sewerage system installed, possibly prompted by a typhoid epidemic. As he was patron of the living, one could say that body, mind and spirit were cared for by the noble Earl.

Agriculture, the base line of the 19th century economy, is still a dominant feature of the environment. Each settlement in the parish is surrounded by farmland, much of it pasture. The difference between then and now is the increase in arable land: the seasons are reflected on a changing patchwork of bare ploughed soil, the green of new growth, the yellow slashes of flowering rape and then the warm tones of ripening grain.

The first commuter, a Northampton shoe manufacturer, came to Brington before the First World War, but commuting is no longer limited to nearby towns. The valley to the south, a communications artery, carries the M1, Watling Street, the London to Glasgow railway and the Grand Union Canal. The latter is now devoted to leisure pursuits, but at times it can be more quickly negotiated than the motorway!

Great Brington

There is a certain nostalgia: for the lost hedgerows and wild flowers; for the slower tempo of life when the bread, baked in the village, was delivered by horse and cart; for some of us, for the pure cold spring water from our own wells; for the brown long-eared bats, whose barn habitats are being developed for humans. Brington's other bat, the pipistrelle, more venturesome has migrated to modern houses.

⌘ BRIXWORTH

The village of Brixworth today is an architectural hotch-potch of ancient stone buildings, Victorian houses, some very pleasing to the eye, and a sprawling mass of modern properties dominated by the now famous ancient church which has stood sentinel on the hill for well over a thousand years.

The remains of a large Roman villa found at Brixworth indicate that a Roman of some importance once lived here. Later the Saxons built a church and Roman tiles may be found incorporated into the fabric of the present building. A sacred relic, said to be part of the larynx of St Boniface, is kept in the church and pilgrims in past ages came to pay homage to the saint or to pray for a miracle. His day, 5th June, has been celebrated with feasts and fetes in the village for centuries.

Brixworth Hall was built in Tudor times. The watercourse we know as 'Merry Tom', where once stood a mill, must have been more of a raging torrent then, unlike the gentle stream where today children paddle and fish for tadpoles. A stone archway and converted stable block are all that remain of the old Hall, built by the Saunders family who owned the mill.

Brixworth is the home of the famous Pytchley Hunt, with grand kennels near the site of the former railway station.

Brixworth became an important coaching stage en route between London and the North. Such was the haste to change horses that at the entrance to one inn yard, with little room for manoeuvre, the stone wall was worn away on one side by the constant friction of passing horseflesh.

In 1851 the railway came to Brixworth, changing the lives of the people as never before. There was now an accelerated drift from the agricultural work that had been their mainstay for centuries. Soon after, iron ore was found and this was to change not only the village, but the contours of the surrounding countryside. There are still those who remember the stories of the hard and dangerous work, the low pay and the heavy drinking, for this was indeed thirsty work. Brick-built cottages sprang up to house the workers, and public houses sprang up to slake their thirst.

After the iron ore was worked out light industry began to take a hold. There is now an expanding industrial estate, built unobtrusively on the edge of the village.

In the centre of the village is an unusual and attractive stone building which is all that remains of the once notorious Brixworth Workhouse. It opened its doors in 1837 and was an unhappy place for the destitute of the parish and beyond. Conditions only began to improve when a farm labourer, not afraid to speak his mind about the unjust treatment, was elected to the Board which administered the workhouse.

The quarries now are gone and the grassy hills and hollows left where the ironstone was removed, echo to the shouts of children at play. One of the artificially created hills makes a wonderful toboggan run!

The conservation areas away from the main road are reminders of the Brixworth of many years ago. There is an ancient butter-cross on the green below the church, the village stocks are now only used by visitors posing for a photograph, and the church of All Saints, magnificent in its simplicity, continues to draw pilgrims and visitors from all over the world.

⌘ CASTLE ASHBY

Castle Ashby is situated on the south side of the flood plain of the river Nene between Northampton and Wellingborough. The Nene forms part of the northern boundary of the parish, while the A428 Northampton–Bedford road approximates to its southern boundary. The 'Castle' part of the name dates from 1306 when Langton, Bishop of Coventry, obtained a licence from the Crown to embattle his mansion at Ashby.

The imposing south gate to Castle Ashby House

Today the village has one of the great houses of Northamptonshire. It is a classic estate village though contrary to what might be expected, most of the buildings are relatively modern. It is clear from such documentary evidence as survives that the village has over the past 200 years been moved from east to west. Today the church, set well to the east of Castle Ashby House, is the only visible indication of this shift. The first stage of this removal appears to have been in 1695 when 'a long stone building near the south side of Ashby church' which had become 'a receptacle for idle persons . . . and a harbour for strumpets . . . woodstealers and vagabonds' was pulled down. In return a new almshouse was built (now 19–24 Castle Ashby).

The second major clearance happened in the 1760s when the area immediately to the north of the house was cleared by Capability Brown in order to create the Dairy Walk. Given that there are no surviving dwellings in the village which clearly date from this period, it would not be unreasonable to suppose that the cottages which were built to replace those that were destroyed were of poor quality.

Most of the existing dwellings date from the 1860s onwards. The most distinguished is 43–46 Castle Ashby, which is date stoned 1874 and is by the Northampton architect E. F. Law. A number of features from this row of cottages – most obviously the gable as an extension of the front wall – were blended with the vernacular tradition to create a distinctive estate style of architecture which can easily be recognised in the surrounding villages. Next door to this row is a school designed by G. E. Street, who was responsible for restoring Castle Ashby church in the 1860s. The reason for his nickname 'Stripey' Street is immediately apparent from this building. Nos 43–46 Castle Ashby and indeed most of the rest of the houses in the village are roofed with tiles made on the estate between about 1880 and 1930. In design they are unique.

⌘ CHACOMBE

Chacombe nestles in a well-wooded valley with hills on all sides except in the direction of Banbury, three miles away. On the road to Middleton Cheney, farmland on either side has been used to make the well-patronised Cherwell Edge Golf Course. On the north side is the county ditch, which, through the centuries, has created its own deep, winding valley; walk over one of its little wooden bridges and you are in Oxfordshire.

On the Banbury road is the Priory, with its medieval chapel. Augustinian monks lived there and several of their fishponds are now the site of the neat, modern village sewerage system, some distance away. The Priory house is a handsome mansion, in a setting of trees, partially surrounded by the original ponds. The nearby Old Vicarage is now a private house and, beyond, the beautiful early 14th century church, set a little apart from today's village, is dedicated to Saint Peter and Saint Paul.

Not far from the church are other carefully restored houses with names reminiscent of their former use: The Old Forge, The Old School, The Old Farmhouse. Bell Cottage probably occupies part of the site of the famous Bagley Bell Foundry (1600–1785) which supplied bells for local church towers and far beyond. Weavers, on the Banbury road, recalls that, for over a century, weaving and plush making was a busy cottage industry.

A field path at Chacombe, looking towards the church of St Peter and St Paul

Silver Street, 60 or so years ago, had three working farms and a wheelwright's shop. Here, only the farmhouses are set back from the street. Most of the other dwellings adjoin the pavement, with no front gardens. There are no working farms in Silver Street now, but the old thatched houses make pleasant homes.

Some of the old names have disappeared too. Silver Street North was once Saucepan Alley, part of the Banbury road was called Catchall, and School Hill was known as Upper Tubs.

⌘ CHARLTON & NEWBOTTLE

Charlton is a small village on the edge of the southern ridge of Northamptonshire. Interestingly, its parish church is situated half a mile away across the fields, at Newbottle, one of Northamptonshire's many deserted villages. All that remains of this medieval settlement, with its beautiful views westward across to north Oxfordshire, are a couple of cottages, the Old Rectory and the Manor, with its striking octagonal dovecote, beside the lovely little church, dating from the 12th century, with a Norman font.

Newbottle made the national press in 1872 when a whirlwind struck. There is a dramatic, well-researched account describing eyewitnesses seeing a 'rope' come down from the heavy storm clouds with a 'ball of smoke' at its base, felling huge trees and knocking down walls along its path, and pulling up the water from a

Newbottle's 12th century church

pond, to deposit it like rain further along. It travelled for nearly two miles, but miraculously nobody was hurt. Newbottle Spinney is now a nature reserve, much visited for its primroses in the spring.

Almost opposite the attractive, thatched Rose & Crown, the last remaining public house of the four that the villagers once had to choose from, stands what must be the grandest cottage in the land. Here lived Charlton's most notable resident – F. E. Smith, the first Earl of Birkenhead, lawyer and statesman, close friend of Churchill and once Lord Chancellor of England. He moved to the 'small hunting box' in 1907 to make a country home for his wife and young family. Over the years "The Cottage' was extended and transformed into an imposing house, unusually, right on the village street, with gardens behind stretching down to a lake. 'F.E.' died in 1930 and his tomb, designed by Lutyens, can be seen in the cemetery to the west of the village.

At intervals along the main street odd blue-brick arched constructions can be seen. These were built through the generosity of Mr F. Myers, a Victorian benefactor living at the Lodge, and provided a piped water supply, the pump house being at the top of Hogg Lane. Four of the original outlets survive – it seems a sophisticated arrangement for a small village, when others had to rely on a single pump, but it had its problems, as early in this century it was reported to the Parish Council that 'children were wasting the water'!

On the southern outskirts of Charlton is Rainsborough Camp, believed to date from the Iron Age, with earth ramparts held by stone walls 2,000 years old, enclosing about six acres. It was later used by the Romans, whose coins have been found in the area.

⌘ COGENHOE

Cogenhoe (pronounced Cookno) is situated six miles east of Northampton, on rising ground overlooking the Nene valley.

The architecture ranges from the Elizabethan rectory to present day buildings, and the earliest dwellings are situated around the village green. The present church building was started about 1225 and completed in 1280 by Nicholas de Cogenhoe, and additions were made by William de Cogenhoe at a later date. The heir to the estate died at the age of 10 and Agnes, his sister and the last of the de Cogenhoe line, built the tower as a memorial to him in about 1380. There are many interesting features in the church including an effigy of a crusader, believed to be Nicholas de Cogenhoe.

During the 19th century many changes took place in the village, with the coming of new trades and occupations. These show up in the church registers, where earlier entries show that most employment was farm work or other rural trades. During the early 1800s you find other job descriptions appearing, eg rail workers, navigators and iron ore miners.

Iron ore was mined in the vicinity during the middle of the 19th century, but the slump in the 1880s proved too much and the company closed in 1888. During the latter half of the 19th century shoemaking was making its mark. Hand-sewn shoes and boots were mostly made in small workshops in the houses. A small factory making high quality boots and shoes was built by the Mann family and this continued to employ local labour until it closed in the late 1940s.

One old lady was a well-known village character. She was married to a man who farmed in a small way, and was fairly comfortably well off, but was so parsimonious she would look through other people's dustbins looking for scraps for her husband's dinner. She was the 'laying out' person in the village and is supposed to have acquired her false teeth from one of the corpses she was attending to. They were much to big for her and she was unable to close her mouth and had a perpetual grin. 'Teeth like gravestones', the villagers used to say!

⌘ COSGROVE

Although Cosgrove is only a few minutes drive from the new city of Milton Keynes over the county boundary, it has retained its village charm. Its geographical position, bounded by the Ouse and Tove rivers, attracted settlers as far back as Roman times.

Cosgrove would have remained relatively isolated until 1805 when the Grand Union Canal was built, bisecting the village. It then found itself not only on the main London to Birmingham route, but also at the junction of the canal arm that led to Buckingham. These days the canal brings visitors in their holiday boats to the village.

More visitors come by road to the leisure park at Cosgrove Lodge, which was formerly the site of a huge sand and gravel pit. It employed many men from the village and surrounding area, but was finally worked out after supplying materials for the stretch of the M1 that runs through north Buckinghamshire and south Northamptonshire.

Cosgrove Priory features in the village's ghost story which is a sad tale concerning the daughter of a family who lived in the house. She fell in love with a shepherd but her family forbade her to see him and, so the story goes, then had the hapless lad deported on a false charge of sheep stealing. Broken-hearted the girl threw herself into the nearby mill race and sometimes at full moon her ghost can be seen in that area.

As well as a ghost, Cosgrove can boast of something more tangible from the past. In a field behind the old National School lies St Vincent's Well, one of the genuine Holy Wells safeguarded by an Act of Parliament. The water is high in iron content and said to have great healing properties, being especially effective in curing eye troubles.

The oldest building in Cosgrove is the church of St Peter and St Paul, with its attractive tower rising high above the houses at the 'top end' of the village. The best view of it is obtained by entering Cosgrove along the Stratford road, past Cosgrove Hall and its pretty thatched lodge. Here in the neighbouring spinney every spring can be seen hundreds of daffodils, which makes this one of the most picturesque spots in the village.

Although Cosgrove has changed and grown over the years, the lack of a through road has helped preserve its air of tranquillity.

⌘ CREATON

Creaton village, lying eight miles north-west of Northampton on the road to Welford, used to be in two parts. Great Creaton and Little Creaton. Now, however, there is little or nothing to be seen of the village that once was Little Creaton and lay a mile or so to the south in Spratton parish. 'Top Orchard' holds its secrets but one or two can still be told. Turn off the Welford road by Highgate House and walk some hundred yards through the Norwegian elms till you near an old stone cottage. Look to your right into the field and call on the ghost of Amphyllis Twigden.

'Top Orchard' was a place she knew well. John Twigden was a yeoman of Little Creaton who married Anne Dickens of Great Creaton, whose family had connections with the Spencers of Althorp and the Thorntons of Brockhall. Anne and John had five daughters, one called Amphyllis. Her early years must have been spent in the gardens and fields around here, her home, now a mere trace, was somewhere just below this turf. She and her four sisters must have walked the path to Spratton church where they had been baptised and as she grew into womanhood she was wooed and won by a man of the church, the Reverend Lawrence Washington of Purleigh. They became the parents of two Virginia emigrants, John and Lawrence.

Well-masoned stones in the field wall and clear lines of foundations in the field betray the old settlement – in living memory some buildings remained there – but only grass grows now where once the Twigden children played.

Point out this place to your friends from the New World; this is where the great-great-grandmother of America's first president, George Washington, was born.

⌘ CULWORTH

Culworth is an ancient site. Stone Age people walked here on an old trackway and a Roman coin has been found in Banbury Lane. A mound and ditch beside the church, known today as Berry Hill, is said to be the remains of a castle built in King Stephen's reign.

St Mary's church dates from the 12th century, but was much restored in 1841. There are six bells in the tower. In the 19th century these were often rung, and an occasion most trying for the inhabitants must have been the hour-long ring starting at 5 am on each Monday in Advent.

St Mary's at Culworth

A product of Culworth was white paving stone which, with blackstone from Byfield, was used to make chequered floors imitating marble, as can be seen in the hall of the manor.

For nearly 20 years in the late 18th century, the notorious Culworth Gang terrorised the countryside for miles around, attacking stagecoaches, robbing travellers and plundering houses. There were about 15 of them, one of the chief being John Smith, described as 'of advanced years, but of great strength and daring'. His two sons also took part as did the parish clerk of Sulgrave (a shoemaker), who was said to carry pistols when about his duties in the church.

They hid much of their booty in Sulgrave church, and for years none dared give evidence against them. Eventually carelessness gave them away. Two members spending the night at an inn at Towcester had two bags with them, said to contain fighting cocks. While they slept the landlord peeped into the bags and found smocks, and blackened masks, which had been the guise of robbers in the district. He told the Constable, and when the villains broke into a house near Blakesley they were caught red-handed. This led to most of the gang being tried at Towcester Assizes in 1787.

Culworth still has a village green, where lies the remains of a stone seat. Until replaced by the war memorial this stood upon a plinth nearby, for the auctioneer on cattle market days.

Deene Hall and the church

⌘ DEENE & DEENETHORPE

As you leave Corby and travel four miles along the road towards Stamford you come across the sister villages of Deene and Deenethorpe. These two are among the last remaining estate villages, both belonging to Deene Park and inhabited by estate workers and old retainers. Deene Park estate has been owned since the 16th century by the Brudenell family, who are descendants of the Earls of Cardigan.

Deene is a tiny, unspoilt limestone village, hiding among the trees on the edge of the Willow Brook to the west of the A43. Deenethorpe is on the opposite side of the main road, nestling on the hillside.

During the Second World War an American air base was located behind Deenethorpe. One night a bomber returning from a raid crashed in the village, damaging properties and shattering the stained glass windows in the Hall. Luckily most of the coloured glass was salvaged and the window has been restored to its former splendour, although the surrounding glass is now clear.

The church of St Peter in Deene was originally built in the 12th century, but was extensively restored in 1868 by Lady Adeline Cardigan in memory of her husband, James – 7th Earl of Cardigan, who was famous for his part in the Battle of Balaclava and the Charge of the Light Brigade.

The 7th Earl was probably the most colourful owner of the estate and the house contains a collection of Crimean memorabilia, including his uniforms and medals. It also houses the stuffed head of the charger *Ronald* that he rode into battle. Lady Adeline, who lived at Deene until 1915, was recalled as being rather eccentric. She wished to be remembered as a beautiful woman, so when her husband died – although she was still comparatively young and outlived him by 46 years – she had her own death mask made at the same time. She kept her coffin in the house and would lie in it and ask people how she looked. Her extravagance finally led to the arrival of the bailiffs and the sale of many of her clothes, carriages and horses. She was often seen bicycling around the village wearing Lord Cardigan's regimental trousers.

⌘ DUDDINGTON

Duddington was originally situated within the old Rockingham Forest and a settlement was recorded in the Domesday survey of 1086.

The approaches to the village are particularly attractive. From the west the road from Leicester crosses the river Welland over an ancient bridge, medieval in origin, and passes by the 17th century watermill with its mansard roofs.

There are many lovely buildings in the village, among them the early 17th century manor. This can be glimpsed from the road through its wrought iron gateways, nestling in its enchanted garden which sweeps down to the banks of the river. Duddington was originally an agricultural community centred on the manor,

The river Welland at Duddington

but although many of the farm buildings remain their usage has changed and most of them are restored as residential properties.

The parish church of St Mary is most notable for its 12th and 13th century architecture and the abnormal siting of its tower – on the south side. This probably occurred because of falling ground on the west wide where the slope to the river begins. Inside there remain some boxed pews, many retaining their 17th century panelling, and a large number of monuments to commemorate the Jackson family from the manor.

The adjacent Church Farm still has a two-cell 18th century dovecote with 800 nesting boxes and from 1775 until 1834 it was the parish workhouse.

⌘ EAST HADDON

In the Domesday Book 'Eddone' is recorded as having three manors each owning 'two ploughs of oxen', with a mill and a church with a clerk, in the gift of the Abbey at Leicester. Church registers later show a pattern of an agricultural peasantry with a population of 300 to 400.

The village appears to have been self-supporting during the 1800s with three large farms employing ten or more men, selling butter, milk and eggs, and a baker, where villagers could also take their Sunday dinner to cook – the signal was

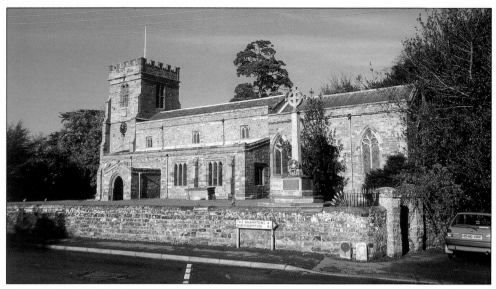

East Haddon church

the tolling of the 'Pudding Bell' (or Sanctus Bell) in the church tower. It was collected at middday, cooked to a turn, and all for 2d! There was also a butcher, a saddler, a dressmaker, and most cottagers had their patch of wheat or barley as well as vegetables and fruit trees. There were at least twelve pumps and many wells.

A 19th century lord of the manor was a Mr Sawbridge who built East Haddon Hall and many cottages for his innumerable staff. He and other public spirited gentlemen endowed the village Church School and a school house in the grounds for the master. There were 87 pupils.

When the railway was built the population rose to 650 and a few more houses were erected. The Co-op and the Methodist chapel were built and the Hall changed ownership. The new lord of the manor was a Member of Parliament with liberal views. He turned one of the inns into a Trust House and encouraged church and chapel to join together in social activities.

East Haddon is a very pretty village with a warm stone towered church, thatched cottages with beautiful gardens and a thatched village pump. Although it is no longer a farming community, it is a lively and 'villagey' place with plenty of activity.

⌘ EASTON MAUDIT

Easton Maudit takes its name from the Maudit family who bought the estate at Easton (East Farm) in 1131. It was not until 1578, however, that the village had its first resident landowner when Sir Christopher Yelverton bought the manor house and estate at Easton. Sir Christopher became Speaker of the House of Commons and his contacts instigated a flow of important visitors over the years.

Easton Maudit vicarage was also the subject of frequent visits. Dr Samuel Johnson, Oliver Goldsmith and David Garrick were often the guests of the then vicar, the Rev Dr Thomas Percy, who was a fellow member of Dr Johnson's London Club – the Garrick. A plaque marks the pew used by them in Easton Maudit church.

An interesting story concerns the Rev Francis Tolson, who was vicar from 1732–45 and is buried in the church. Apparently he was not wrapped in wool at his interment according to the then laws of England; a practice designed to help the farmers of the day! Through this neglect he could not rest in his grave and it was said that he 'walked' at night by the pond in the vicarage garden. He is said to have been eventually laid to rest by twelve clergymen throwing 13 lighted candles into the pond after him so that the ghost could not walk again until the candles were burnt out!

⌘ EASTON-ON-THE-HILL

Easton-on-the-Hill is situated in the very north-eastern tip of the county of Northamptonshire, on the borders of Cambridgeshire, Lincolnshire and that part of Leicestershire that was Rutland.

A lane lined by small limestone houses, topped with Collyweston slate roofs, leads up the hill to the church, standing among trees in the churchyard. The parish church of All Saints is the dominant landmark of the village and dates back to the 12th century, but it has been enlarged and altered over the centuries. Some of the pews have been there since Stuart times and retain the oak pegs where men hung their hats while they were at prayer. Before the organ was installed the hymn singing was accompanied by a long bassoon – housed in the vestry. There is also a tablet to the memory of Lancellot Skinner – a rector's son who was lost in the famous wreck of *La Lutine* off the coast of Holland in 1799. The ship's bell was recovered and has become historic in the City of London, hanging at Lloyds.

The oldest building in the village is the 'Priests House'. Formerly the Old Rectory it was built around 1500, but probably ceased to be a clergy house as early as 1553. It was then used as stables, extensively repaired in 1867, and finally passed to the National Trust.

In the early part of the 20th century a great many men were employed at the Easton-on-the-Hill ironstone quarry. This was only operational for about 50 years and it was never a great success, probably due to the fact that the closest ironworks were in Scunthorpe and the inclining ground made working the site very restrictive. They did, however, enjoy a few years of prosperity during the First World War when the demand for iron was at its peak.

⌘ EVENLEY

The village of Evenley stands on elevated ground about a mile south-east of Brackley. It lies near the point of junction of the three parishes of Turweston, Evenley and Mixbury and of the three counties of Buckinghamshire, Northamptonshire and Oxfordshire.

For visitors to Evenley the first impression is that created by the village green, which is roughly square and is bounded by a roadway on all four sides. The green is flat and the turf is well tended, providing an area for children's recreation and well suited for cricket.

The manor house situated near to the north-west corner of the green is one of the oldest buildings in the village. Diagonally opposite at the south-west corner stands the Red Lion Hotel. At one time there was a roadway between these two buildings to give easy access out of the village for horse-drawn vehicles. This roadway was later taken over by the County Council, closed and grassed over. In a very hot summer the route of the old road can be clearly seen as a band of parched grass.

The Anglican church of St George is located to the north-west of the village. The original building may have been Norman or Saxon in origin. Almost all records of Evenley in early times perished in a fire that gutted the church. The present church is a stone structure in the Early English style and was rebuilt in 1865 at the expense of the Hon Mrs Pierrepont of Evenley Hall in memory of her husband.

The Hall is set back some distance from the A43 and is reached by way of an avenue lined with lime trees. Viewed from a distance these trees look like a row of

Evenley's spacious village green

guards wearing busbies! During the Second World War the Hall was used by the Yorkshire Regiment. In 1941 ownership passed to the trustees of the National Children's Home and after the war the premises were adapted for the residential care of children.

⌘ EVERDON

Everdon is situated about two miles south of the A45. It has grown in a valley, surrounded by rolling countryside, having the beautiful woodlands of Mantles Heath and Everdon Stubbs nearby. Visitors from many miles away come each spring to see the bluebells in all their glory.

The village is old. It is mentioned in a charter dated AD 944, and at the time of the Domesday Book (1086) it belonged to the Bishop of Bayeaux. Later, much of Everdon was the property of the Benedictine abbey of Bernay in Normandy.

Like London and Northampton, Everdon has had its Great Fire. This occurred on 13th April 1786 when a serious fire broke out at 2 pm. In a short time it had engulfed some 20 houses as well as outhouses and workshops. It spread rapidly across the thatched roofs, but fortunately there was no loss of life. Both College Farm and the Stone House still have scorch marks on beams in their roofs.

The poet Thomas Gray frequently stayed at Everdon Rectory with his uncle, the Reverend William Antrobus, who was rector here from 1729 to 1744. Many believe that it is Everdon churchyard rather than Stoke Poges churchyard which was the inspiration for his *Elegy*.

St Mary's is a huge church for a village the size of Everdon, more akin to one of the Suffolk 'Wool Churches'. It is thought that prosperous local people combined with the monks from Bernay to build this fine place of worship. It is constructed partly of local ironstone, which, although lovely to look at, weathers badly, and much repair and restoration has had to be carried out in recent years.

The south aisle is said to have been reserved for the parishioners of Snorscombe. The manor house, now a disused farmhouse, one cottage and a converted mill are all that remain of this once flourishing community. The village was depopulated and its houses pulled down by order of Richard Knightly of Fawsley in 1520.

⌘ EYDON

The small and attractive village of Eydon lies close to the centre of England, in the southern corner of Northamptonshire. It is well positioned on a hill, surrounded by idyllic undulating countryside. The village contains many fine historic buildings, including Eydon Hall, built by Francis Annesley in 1788 and designed by James Lewis.

Eydon was recorded in the Domesday Book in 1086, but it is thought by some to

The village pump at Eydon

have been inhabited long before this. Whatever its Saxon origin, it grew at the side of the ancient Roman road from the villa at Chipping Warden to a settlement at Daventry.

It is believed that a church has been standing in Eydon since 1154. The present building has a Norman font and 14th century tower. Although the medieval records for Eydon are not complete, some of the villagers must have been quite wealthy because the church records show generous gifts at this time. The village suffered two fires, the first being on 13th August 1651, the second on 28th May 1905. Some of the stone in the village buildings even today show the scorch marks from the fires.

The railways brought welcome alternative employment in the 19th century for the villagers, with the Central and East and West junction railways running close by the village. Apart from work and some prosperity, the railways also brought cheaper coal and newspapers on the day of publication! People were very keen to read of the latest news during the Boer War because three Eydon men were fighting in the armed forces. The railways gradually went into decline and on the 4th September 1966 it was all over. The last train passed by, leaving Eydon with a great silence.

In recent years there has been renewed interest in Eydon, partly due to the ease of communication offered by the M40 motorway away to the west.

Farthinghoe from the Millennium Green

⌘ FARTHINGHOE

Farthinghoe is five miles from Banbury and three miles from Brackley, within reach of Northampton and Oxford. The village is split by the A422, along which huge lorries travel at high speed, at times barely negotiating the very sharp corner at the end of the village.

Architecturally it is a mixture of old and new. The main building is the church of St Michael and All Angels. The tower is Norman, and was repaired by Sir John Egerton in 1654 – the date being carved under the one-handed clock, which is quite an unusual feature. In 1443 John Abbott founded a school in the vestry, which was then a chantry chapel.

Next to the church is the village's oldest and most interesting house, Abbey Lodge. It dates from the 15th century, with later alterations. It has a fine carved and moulded fireplace and on the north side a newel stair leading to the upper chamber. Being so old it has a ghost, heard but not seen!

⌘ FOTHERINGHAY

The first written mention of Fotheringhay was in 1060, and it is listed in the Domesday Book in 1086 as 'Fodringeia'.

Fotheringhay from the river Nene

After many different owners, the manor came into the possession of Edward III who gave it to his son Edmund Langley, the first Duke of York and founder of that powerful house. It was he who founded the College whose chaplains and choristers were to pray for the souls of the founders and their families. Edmund's son Edward Langley continued the work until he was killed at Agincourt in 1415. His body was brought home and buried in the choir, although it was not finished until about 1430. To this private, collegiate church was added the parish church in the same style, begun in 1434. This is the only part which remains today.

Fotheringhay is most famous for the birth of Richard III at the castle in 1452, and for the trial and beheading of Mary, Queen of Scots in 1587. At the time of Richard's birth Fotheringhay had become one the principal seats of his parents, Richard Plantagenet and Cecily Neville, Duke and Duchess of York, and he spent his first six years here. Members of the Richard III Society join villagers at the annual carol service, and have given a memorial window to the church and refurbished the chapel in memory of the House of York.

Mary Stuart was brought here in September 1586 after 18 years in captivity in different safe places and prisons in other parts of England. Her trial took place in the Great Hall of the castle on 14th and 15th of October and she was beheaded on 8th February 1587.

The castle does not seem to have been used after Mary's death. It fell into ruins and was pulled down in 1635. The stones have been used to build many cottages and walls around the village.

⌘ GAYTON

Gayton stands on high ground to the south-west of Northampton, with fine views to the east and west.

In the past much ironstone was mined in the area, which has left some of the roads high above the surrounding fields. National Steel developed iron ore excavation in a large way but soon closed owing to the increased railway charges for transporting the ore to the furnaces. On the ground sloping towards the river Nene were, at one time, three brickyards.

Travelling south-west from the village on still rising ground one comes to the highest point – a flat, clay, waterlogged land with the watershed of the river Nene to the north and the river Ouse to the south. There by the wayside of the road to Eastcote is Millmott, where there was once a watermill. The site is surrounded by high and ancient willow trees and a large deep drain ditch still remains around a hardcore centre.

In the village by the five roads called Five Ways is a small green known as The Pound, originally a wall-surrounded place for impounding stray cattle.

To the north-east of the village is the parish church of St Mary the Virgin. In 1815 the church was restored from its ruinous state by the Rev Dr Butler, but the tower was not reconstructed to its former great height. Standing on high ground it must have once have been a noticeable landmark from the upper Nene valley. A further restoration was carried out in 1881–83 by Rev. J. C. Williams Ellis, when the chancel was rebuilt and the organ chamber and vestry added.

One of the several tombs in the church is the 14th century one of Lady Scholastica, daughter of Sir Philip de Gayton, who is reputed to have murdered

Gayton village

her husband. The child Mabilla, cradled between the corbels above the tomb, is not her child but that of her sister, Julianna de Murdak, who was burned as a witch.

In the past, as in most villages, Gayton had its own blacksmith, builder, carpenter, baker, shopkeeper, tailor and dressmaker – but alas none today. Opposite the Pound is a very attractive thatched cottage which was once the home of the local cooper, or barrel-maker.

⌘ GEDDINGTON

Geddington lies on the main A43, three miles from Kettering and three miles from Corby. One of the treasures of the village is the Cross, built in 1294 as a memorial to Edward I's beloved Queen Eleanor. He built a cross at each resting place of her funeral procession from Nottinghamshire to London. Geddington Cross is one of the three surviving and is thought to be the best, both in architectural purity and

The river Ise at Geddington

preservation. The bridge is older than the Cross by 40 years and travellers today may cross the river Ise the same way that Queen Eleanor's cortege crossed more than 700 years ago.

The church of St Mary Magdelene which received the body of the Queen overnight was then many centuries old. At the rear of the church was a medieval royal hunting palace. Nothing of this now remains except for some fragments of stone in the church, but it is possible that the steeply buttressed cottages in Wood Street originate from the same period. The name Wood Street emphasises the reason for a palace in Geddington, for this was the heart of Rockingham Forest and very popular with kings and courts of the Middle Ages.

⌘ GRAFTON UNDERWOOD

Grafton Underwood lies in the north of the county, and is located about four miles east of the town of Kettering. It is referred to in the Domesday Book as Grastone. The 'Underwood' was added in the 18th century, probably referring to Grafton Park Wood, part of the old Rockingham Forest which is nearby.

A small stream, a tributary of the river Nene, crossed by several bridges, runs down the side of the main street. The majority of the stone cottages are on the east side of the stream, some of these set at right angles to the road, which gives a pleasing appearance. The cottages are mostly 17th and 18th century, and quite a few of the roofs are thatched, intermingled with Collyweston slate and pantiles. The manor house, dated 1653, is also on the east side.

On the west side of the stream there are some green open spaces and paddocks, with several fine chestnut trees, that afford pleasant views of the parish church of St James. The old school and schoolhouse also lies on the west side. Erected in 1853 by the then Duke of Buccleuch, it is now a private home.

The church is a mixture of various architectural designs and periods. The oldest parts are the tower and the nave, which are late Norman. In the vestry there is a record of Thomas Carley, 1757–1825. He was born without hands, and later went on to be parish clerk and schoolmaster. A sample of his copperplate writing can be seen. He held the pen in his mouth.

A recent addition is a stained glass window, dedicated to the memory of the 1,579 members of the American Eighth Air Force who gave their lives while serving at Grafton Underwood airfield during the Second World War, and especially the members of the 384th Bombardment Group (heavy) who served there the longest.

The airfield to the north of the village was built in 1941. It has the distinction of having been the airfield from which the first and last bombing raid by the American Eighth Air Force in Europe took off. A granite memorial has been erected on the airfield by the 384th Group, and in addition a banner was presented to the village. It now hangs in the village hall.

⌘ GREAT ADDINGTON

Great Addington or 'Addington Magna' is a small village situated four miles south-west of Thrapston, bordered on the east by Ringstead, the south by Little Addington and the west by Burton Latimer. The village is situated in a prominent position overlooking the river Nene.

There is an ancient burial ground near the south-east end of the village. This elevation has always been known as Shooters Hill, and was used by the ancient Britons and Romans. In the spring of 1847, a Mr Cole writes: 'whilst digging for gravel the spades of men employed came into contact with many perfect skeletons. There was no indication that a tumulus had been erected to protect them, the sand and gravel proving admirable preservatives. In some cases the face of the body had been placed downwards, others laid on their side, whilst three were recorded indicating rudely constructed urns or vases of unbaked clay, known as drinking cups, indications of Druid Influences.'

The church in Great Addington is dedicated to All Saints. The earliest recorded history of the church mentions that the manor and certain arable lands were given to the Abbey of Croyland in AD 829 by Wonoth. There is a possible mention from a charger of AD 833 of a church at Great Addington in the 12th century. A Norman church existed on the present site, but of that building only the south porchway remains. The church was dedicated in 1234; alterations followed, including the building of the tower in 1350.

Within the church is a tomb with an alabaster figure of Henry de Vere Esq who

All Saints' church at Great Addington

died in 1516, the last of his particular line. Previously, in 1125, an Audrey de Vere dwelt in the manor, which through him passed to his second son Robert de Vere. Eventually Henry de Vere inherited the manor and lands in the time of Henry VII. He had lived through the War of the Roses, fought on Bosworth Field and possessed two printed books.

The manor house where de Vere lived was thought to be situated somewhere near the present Home Farm. However, today's manor house stands near the church and is of Jacobean origin.

Employment in the village in 1840 was basically agriculture – six farmers are mentioned in the Gazetteer of Northamptonshire. One of these farmers, a Thomas Coleman, was also a miller, the cornmill being situated behind the present Home Farm. Another mill – probably a papermill – was situated towards Ringstead station. Other occupations recorded were, apart from the rector, a carpenter, a victualler, a blacksmith, a wheelwright and shopkeeper.

Recollections of the village in the 1920s reveal that agriculture was still the principal employment; people also remember a blacksmith's shop and two pubs, the Hare and Hounds and the Leopard. There were two shops, one adjoining the bakehouse kept by Ginger Wilson, where you could get a Sunday dinner cooked for 2d. The other, kept by a Mrs Warr, was a general store and generally in a muddle. A chimney sweep, Fred Smith, was in residence, and there was Wesleyan chapel with services on Sunday and a reading room/concert hall in the week, but strictly teetotal.

⌘ GREAT BILLING

In common with other villages in the immediate vicinity of Northampton, Great Billing has been enveloped by the expansion of the county town. However, there are still villagers who can remember it consisting of one main street running from the Wellingborough road to Billing station, with footpaths across the meadows to Ecton, Little Billing and Weston Favell.

The village is listed in the Domesday Book, and up to the 14th century was situated to the west of the parish church. The population was then decimated by the Black Death, and they abandoned the old village and rebuilt it gradually in its present location. It is fortunate that parts of the village retain much of the old atmosphere, centring on the 12th century church of St Andrew and the old rectory. The old village pump and horse trough can still be seen, and there are several other notable buildings in both Church Way and Elwes Way.

The story of Great Billing is intertwined with that of the Elwes family, who at one time owned the whole of the village with the exception of one house and five cottages. They lived in Billing Hall, built in 1776 and unfortunately demolished in 1956.

The only tangible links between the family and the village remaining today are the names of the village inn, the Elwes Arms, and two roads named after members of the family, Elwes Way and Lady Winefrides's Walk.

The expansion of the village has changed both the pace of life and the composition of the population, but older villagers thinking of earlier times remember such characters as Charlie Tipler, the village sweep and lay preacher. He was always smartly dressed with a clean shirt and shining face. His mode of transport was pony and trap. He was a great conversationalist, with tales of chimney sweeping in the past at Billing Hall and Horton House. Unfortunately when talking he ignored the passing of time, so that no matter what time he was due villagers learned to expect him only when they could hear the sound of his horse's hoofs!

When outsiders think of Billing today they often first call to mind the Aquadrome, created from old gravel workings. However, a link between the new and old remains within its grounds: Billing Mill, now a museum, where villagers used to take their corn to be ground.

⌘ GREAT DODDINGTON

Great Doddington is a long narrow village which lies between Wellingborough town and the village of Earls Barton. It is thought that it dates back to the Iron Age, since traces of four hut circles, storage pits and an internal ditch have been discovered. Quantities of Saxon and Roman pottery have also been found near the village. There is a limestone ridge, hence the road leading into the village is named The Ridge and the village is built mainly of grey limestone, unlike surrounding villages.

In Church Lane, the centre of the village, stands lovely St Nicholas' church, which is partly Norman. One of its fascinating features is a Jacobean pulpit with a wrought iron hourglass dated 1618. Of the four misericords, one of the carvings shows the artists at work carving the rosettes which adorn the seats. Also in Church Lane is the Old Vicarage, a listed building, no longer a vicarage and now privately owned. At the top of the lane is Doddington Manor Farm, a splendid old manor house.

Hardwater Mill is a very pretty picture and a popular attraction for visitors. It is said that the Archbishop of Canterbury, Thomas à Becket, fled here after a clash with King Henry II at Northampton Castle. He was sheltered by the miller before going into self-imposed exile in France. The mill is now converted into a private house.

⌘ GREATWORTH

Greatworth is situated on a hill, some 500 ft up, and lies just to the south of an important old drove road, Welsh Lane, used for taking stock from Wales to London.

The houses on the west side of The Street were originally part of the hamlet of Westhorp, administered by Marston St Lawrence. In 1935 Westhorp became part of Greatworth. Before that the old minute books of both parishes record many disputes between them. Village folk in Westhorp had to be buried in Marston churchyard and it is recorded that in 1895 a bier was purchased to convey the corpses the one and a half miles down the steep hill to Marston, despite the fact that Greatworth church was only a few hundred yards away.

The layout of the village is such that the houses, old farmsteads and terraced rows of cottages form tight building lines winding along the natural contours and creating attractive streetscapes. The older part contains a number of listed buildings. The row of houses known as Dering Cottages remind us of Lady Dering, who seems to have been an early supporter of education for women, as she endowed a charity for girls as well as boys which still gives small grants to students from the village.

The manor house has a commanding position overlooking the agricultural landscape. The present manor stands on the site of the two previous manors, the second of which was destroyed by fire in 1793 along with many of the village records. The pair of elaborately carved stone pineapple finials still stand marking the entrance of the previous building. George Washington, America's first president, was descended from the Pargeter family of Greatworth.

'A little wayside church' is how Arthur Mee described the village church of St Peter. The battlemented tower is 15th century but the chancel is 13th century and the nave has been rebuilt in the style of the first English builders. In the churchyard a magnificent sycamore tree and a healthy old hornbeam stand among some very old gravestones.

'A little wayside church' – St Peter's at Greatworth

Between Cockley Hill and Greatworth lies Cockley Brake. This is the overgrown remains of early Victorian enterprise, the junction of the Banbury to Bletchley and the Banbury to Northampton railway lines. The second route was not all that successful commercially, but in its latter days the lads of the village would stand by the track to hear the Northampton football score called out by the driver, and to catch the newspapers thrown to them for delivery in the village.

Geographically the area is a watershed with streams running into three rivers, the Ouse, the Cherwell and the Tove. The fact that the village stands on one of the highest points in Northamptonshire accounts for the presence of RAF Greatworth to the north of the village. The tall masts, ugly in close-up but a landmark for miles, are now redundant.

⌘ GREENS NORTON

Situated two miles from Towcester, Greens Norton is a pleasant and attractive village containing old houses and cottages built of the local yellow stone, as well as more modern developments. It was once well known for its lacemakers.

The village is dominated by the tall slender spire of St Bartholomew's church, which is a landmark for miles around. A church was standing on the site in the 9th century but little of this is still visible as so much has been added over the

Yellow stone cottages at Greens Norton

centuries . . . and removed, too. There is a peal of six bells in the tower and this is rung regularly. By the belfry door hangs the coat of arms of Queen Elizabeth I, thought to be a rarity as Cromwell's armies often destroyed such things.

Opposite the church is the Chantrey House, where priests used to live who were occupied in the affairs of the church, taking services at altars in the side aisles.

The big old rectory, hidden behind the church (and now a private house), boasts two ghosts, a tall lady and . . . a pair of legs! It has been suggested that a floor level has been altered at some time to account for this odd phenomenon.

The centre of the village, marked by its green, has not changed too much over the past 60 or so years as the old substandard cottages, which have been demolished, were in yards off the main street, and most new housing has been built on the outskirts.

The oldest house in the village has the date 1666 carved on the chimney but as a priest hole has been found within the house, it would seem to be much older, probably early 16th century. Catherine Parr, sixth wife of Henry VIII, is said to have lived there and to have visited the rectory.

The original village school, which was a dame school, is still standing at the head of School Lane. Its successor, a red brick Victorian building in the High Street, is now in use as the village hall, itself having been replaced by a modern school.

In recent years a 'Pocket Park' has been created on the site of the old brickyard, about a quarter of a mile down a track from the village. The area has been cleared and fenced and about 150 trees planted, including many oaks, though in early summer the site is a riot of dog roses.

⌘ GUILSBOROUGH

Guilsborough has always been a lively place in which to live, with many dramatic happenings throughout the centuries. Beautifully situated at 500 ft above sea level, close to two large, most decorative reservoirs, with sailing and fishing, it is a very old village. In one house there are the remains in the cellar of a Saxon dwelling, roughly dated at AD 867, and there was an extensive Roman encampment in the area, part of which is still visible.

In 1612 scandal ran riot over a case of witchcraft, when two unfortunate Guilsborough women were hanged for bewitching into grievous bodily harm a certain Mrs Belcher and her brother-in-law. Before their demise one of them, joined by two others, rode forth upon a sow's back to visit another powerful old witch residing at Ravensthorpe. This interesting scene is depicted on the arresting banner which hangs in the village hall!

In 1645, during the Civil War, General Thomas Fairfax camped here before the battle of Naseby, and one can imagine him and his soldiers marching down Nortoft Hill in colourful battle array on that morning of 14th June.

The Domesday Book mentions a church in Guilsborough, though there are now no traces left of this Saxon building. The church of St Etheldreda (once dedicated to St Wilfred) was mostly built in the 13th century, with later additions.

The grammar school is the most handsome building in the village, a magnificent example of Jacobean architecture in apricot coloured Northamptonshire stone. It was opened in 1668 to 'provide free eduction for 50 youths within a radius of four miles'. It is said that some of the masters used to reside in the house just across the road from the school, which remained operative as such until 1909. It has now been converted into five attractive dwellings, which preserve the beautiful exterior.

This is hunting country and the many lovely, old houses in Guilsborough have, over the years, provided sturdy supporters for the local Pytchley Hunt. It is a regular, thrilling sight to see riders and hounds surging down the High Street en route to a meet.

⌘   HACKLETON, HORTON & PIDDINGTON

The three close-knit villages of Hackleton, Horton and Piddington lie on the south-east border of the county, in the shadows of Salcey Forest. Their origins lie deep in history. A Roman villa has been excavated at Piddington showing that there was a settlement there in Roman time. When the Domesday survey was carried out in the 11th century, William the Conqueror's niece, Countess Judith, is said to have owned the land around the three villages.

Horton church is adorned by the alabaster tomb of Sir William Parr and his wife Mary. Their niece, Catherine Parr, was the sixth wife of Henry VIII. Horton is also know to have been the birthplace of Charles Montagu, 1st Earl of Halifax, who established the Bank of England in 1694.

Hackleton's claim to history lies with William Carey and the Baptist chapel dedicated to his memory. He was the first Baptist missionary and lived and worked in both Hackleton and Piddington as a cobbler. He called the little cobbler's shop at Hackleton 'Carey's College', and it was from here that he walked six miles to be baptised in the river Nene. Night after night he would read about the voyages of Captain Cook and this kindled the fire of his missionary work, which eventually took him to India.

Hackleton was once a hamlet of the parish of Piddington and hence has no parish church. In 1709, however, the Northampton to Stoke Goldington turnpike road was opened, bypassing Piddington, which subsequently diminished in importance while Hackleton thrived and is now the hub of the community.

The surrounding countryside offers a wealth of flora and fauna with interesting walks into the nearby forest and to neighbouring villages. Wherever you walk there are ever-changing views of Piddington church visible from miles around, a welcoming and friendly beacon as you tread your way home.

⌘ HARGRAVE

Hargrave is a small village lying just inside Northamptonshire on the boundaries of Bedfordshire and Cambridgeshire. During the Roman occupation of Britain there was a settlement here, the name Hargrave means 'the army camp', and several stone coffins dating from that period have been unearthed in the area and are on display outside the church.

In the 19th century Hargrave had a thriving clay pit and brickworks, used for building the local houses. The clay pit is now a pond and the brickworks are ruins which are supposed to be haunted! At that time most of the village inhabitants were employed as farm labourers but others were shepherds, shoemakers and lacemakers. There used to be many shops in the village and the names of the older houses reflect their past uses – Forge House, The Old Bakehouse, Cobblers and The Old Post Office. The track of the old disused railway line between Kettering and Cambridge is still partly visible in farmland near the village outskirts; the nearest local station was at Raunds. On the Bedfordshire side of the village near to a farm, named after it, is the site of Hargrave Mill, now lying in ruins, but at one time producing flour for the village bakery.

At the entrance to Hargrave on the main A45 road stands a house beside a water-tower called Three Shire House, so named became that is where the three counties actually meet. In 1837 the owner was an eccentric old farmer whose wife died suddenly. For various reasons it was impossible to have her buried at Hargrave church. The farmer then refused to have her buried at all, but had the body bricked up in the house, and when his daughter died in 1843 he placed her

Hargrave

body beside that of her mother. It was only 24 years later, when the old farmer himself died, that his surviving son buried the bodies in a neighbouring churchyard.

At one time there was a Methodist chapel in Brook Street, but this closed in the 1960s leaving only the small but picturesque church of All Hollows, or All Saints as it is generally called. The present church dates from the late 12th century although evidence of an earlier wooden church has been found at the site. It was extensively restored in 1869 and is now a listed building.

⌘ HARRINGTON

Harrington, recorded in the Domesday Book as Arintone, is a quiet, unspoiled village, about seven miles west of Kettering, on a hill above the Ise valley with wonderful views over miles of open countryside.

Behind the chestnut trees in the middle of the village is the Falls Field, once the site of a monastic manor owned by the Knights Hospitallers of St John of Jerusalem and later laid out as an ornamental garden with fishponds, sunken gardens and terraces. The site has been carefully preserved and the fishponds are some of the finest in the county.

The Tollemache Arms takes its name from the Rev Hugh Tollemache, who was rector of Harrington for 58 years and died in 1890 at the age of 87. He objected to villagers attending the pub on Sundays so he bought the public house, took it over and installed his coachman as landlord closing the inn from Saturday night until Monday morning.

A short distance from the village down the lane leading to Thorpe Underwood is the 13th century church of St Peter and St Paul, originally dedicated to St Botolph. This is a listed building. In a glass case at the west end of the church is an ancient wind instrument known as a vamping horn, one of only eight still surviving in the country, two of them in Northamptonshire. It is thought to originate from the 17th century and may have been used as a primitive loudspeaker trumpet to 'vamp' an accompaniment for hymns and psalms.

By the side of the road to Lamport is an impressive modern memorial to American airmen who lost their lives in the Second World War. The crews known as the 'Carpetbaggers' flew hazardous night bombing missions from this secret base, also dropping munitions and supplies and parachuting agents to underground resistance forces in Nazi-occupied Europe.

⌘ HELLIDON

The village of Hellidon, reputedly one of the highest in Northamptonshire, lies adjacent to the Warwickshire border in the southern part of the county. The rivers Leam, Cherwell and Nene rise in or around the village.

The church, which is dedicated to St John the Baptist, lies at the centre of the village. A date over the entrance door proclaims that it was built in 1591, although the tower is older and is said to have been built in about 1350, whilst the north aisle and chancel were added at later dates in the 19th century. The four bells were hung in 1615 and 1635. They came from the foundry of Hugh Watts and were rehung in 1860. During the Second World War when the church bells remained silent, bees made over one hundredweight of honey in the clock works.

The windmill, situated at the eastern end of the village, has long since lost its sails and been converted to a private home. It was probably around the turn of the century that the last sacks of flour were milled there. The miller himself lived in what is now the only thatched house in the village.

At the eastern boundary of the parish there is still some evidence of the once productive ironstone quarries which closed in 1961. The ironstone system was connected with the Grand Central Railway by a small branch line which ran for $3/4$ mile parallel to the road until it reached Charwelton station.

Although the building of the Grand Central Railway in 1895 did not much affect Hellidon – it passed under the parish rather than across its land – there are four men buried in the churchyard who died in the construction of the tunnel, which at $1^3/4$ miles in length was the longest on the line, and took just over two years to construct. The necessity of a tunnel was because the owner of nearby Catesby House would not allow a railway line across his parkland – it therefore had to be put beneath it.

Hellidon village

⌘ HINTON IN THE HEDGES

Hinton in the Hedges lay on the main route between Banbury and Brackley until the 18th century, when the Banbury to Buckingham turnpike was built. Nowadays Hinton is some distance from a main road and people visit it more by desire than by necessity.

In the way of many villages, Hinton has grown up around the church, and the small triangular green close by is still its centre. The old rectory on the north side of the green is a building of substance and Manor Farm just off the south-east corner is the largest of the four old farmhouses within the nucleus of the village. In the 1960s many of the old cottages and Lord Crewe's almshouses were in a poor state of repair but since then much renovation has taken place, new houses have been built and a number of old barns have been converted into houses. Other buildings besides the barns have changed their use, and some have fallen into disuse: the old school and the village shop are now houses, the smithy is a garage and the malthouse a ruin.

The green is the focal point of the village but it has no special function because of its small size. An old village pump stands on it and so does an oak seat where children often congregate. Local Morris men come here by tradition to perform the Morris dance which originated in Hinton. From the green it is only a short step to quench their thirst at the Crewe Arms! The village pub is an attractive old building and it fulfils an important role in the community as a social centre.

The green at Hinton in the Hedges

Hinton church lies in a quiet churchyard at the end of a drive running up from the north side of the green. Traces of Saxon masonry suggest that the building replaced an earlier simpler church. The present church, built of limestone, has a nave, chancel, north aisle and a Romanesque tower which leans to the west in a rather picturesque way.

⌘ ISLIP

The picturesque village of Islip stands on high ground on the west bank of the river Nene. Approaching from Thrapston you will cross the 12th century 'nine arch' bridge, originally a packhorse bridge. Set back behind a high stone-faced wall lies Islip House, which is often floodlit by night. This was the home of Thomas Squire, who played a large part in making the river navigable from Peterborough to Thrapston. The grand opening was in November 1737. At that time wharves had been built on both sides of the river and the old warehouses still exist today. Beneath Islip House were the bonded wine vaults.

In the High Street most buildings are of Northamptonshire limestone, many being thatched and presenting a charm of their own. School Lane is a short cul de sac with several interesting houses including the old rectory, and terminated by very old farm buildings, indicating the original function of the village. Also here is St Nicholas' church, parts of which date back to the 12th century.

Islip from the river Nene

View to Islip church across the river Nene

Beside the village hall stands what was a row of very old cottages, which were virtually derelict until refurbished and made into a delightful dwelling. Beyond this lies the working men's club, which back in the days of horsepower was a horse collar factory, and has since played an important role in village life.

In Mill Road there is a thatched cottage called 'The Old Shop' which was in use within living memory, but now is a private dwelling. Near this is a narrow three-storeyed red brick building with a bay window. This was once the home of the manager of the other horse collar factory, which stood behind and to the side, but was demolished for housing. It is said that at that time there was no bay window and the factory owner's wife dearly wanted one, but he saw no reason to waste money on such trivialities. However, he was called away on business to London and upon his return he was greeted with this window!

The old mill was there in the early 1700s, as records show that Thomas Squire leased it whilst working on the navigation project. It continued to grind corn right up to 1960. It is now a private residence and is in remarkably good preservation. A narrow footbridge crosses the river at this point, over the parish border into Thrapston.

⌘ KELMARSH

Kelmarsh is a small village situated in the Northamptonshire uplands. The village itself is to the north and east of the crossroads formed by the A508 and the by-roads leading to Clipston and Harrington. Lovely stone cottages line the east side of the main road, and more of red brick are on the north side of the road to Harrington.

It is difficult to believe the tragedy which overtook the stone cottages on the 4th May 1943. On that day, as lunch was being prepared, a spark somehow ignited the thatched roof of the middle house. A strong wind was blowing, and all the 13 houses were destroyed, rendering 44 people homeless. No one was injured, but few possessions were rescued. The cottages were rebuilt in their present form in 1948.

One of the first line of cottages on the Harrington road has a porch. This was the first school in Kelmarsh, built in 1850. Evidently there was trouble in the village in 1849 and Lord Bateman, owner of the village and occupant of Kelmarsh Hall, gave all his tenants notice because they had lapsed into bad habits. They were called to the Hall where they were told to attend church regularly and live in peace with each other, conducting themselves honestly and soberly. A school would be built so that children would learn to read, write and sum, and a charge of 1d per child per week would be made. Notices would be withdrawn if the tenants signed an agreement promising to behave themselves in the future!

The church, dedicated to St Denys, is a short distance from the village on the road to Clipston. As with most village churches it goes back far into history, but was altered considerably in 1874 by the Naylor family, who were the owners of the village at that time. It is now in the grand Victorian manner, unusual in a village church.

Kelmarsh Hall is a beautifully proportioned building of mellow red brick. It was built in 1728–32 by Francis Smith of Warwick to the design of James Gibbs for Mr William Hanbury, a noted antiquarian.

⌘ KINGS CLIFFE

Kings Cliffe, 14 miles west of Peterborough was noted in the old days for wooden ware – and is known as the wooden spoon village. The men had lathes in their backyards and lovely pieces of work were made.

There is a large village hall and a church room which is used for many activities. This room was originally part of the old watermill and the sluice water can sometimes be heard, which tends to drown the proceedings! The church room holds the archives of the village, with pictures and photos of every part of village life.

The library of William Law is housed in the Library House on School Hill. William Law was born in the village, the son of a grocer. He was a non-juror – a clergyman of great standing – who never became rector of a parish. He helped the poor and was instrumental in founding the Law and Hutchinson Almshouses for six or seven widows or single ladies. These are near the old school where both boys and girls attended, around 2d a week paying for their education. The girls wore

Kings Cliffe from the Willow Brook

bonnets made of a cotton material, and aprons. The old school is still preserved with the master's desk in one corner. In Bridge Street are the Cornforth Homes, endowed by a wealthy lady of the village.

The Miles family were timber merchants and great trees were brought to the big wood yard near the station. The Miles property was later a youth hostel and crowds of cyclists would be seen around the village in the 1930s.

The Second World War brought American airmen to the big aerodrome on the Wansford road near the village. Some of the local girls married and went back to America after the war. The great number of children who came to the village as evacuees must remember the days at 'Cliffe now they are grown up.

⌘ KINGS SUTTON

Although a large village, Kings Sutton is quiet and peaceful. The heart of the village is The Square with the church of St Peter and St Paul on the west side and the 17th century manor on the south-west corner. The 16th century court house is now occupied as a private dwelling. Lovells, a large residence which presumably owes its name to the 14th century lords of the manor, is also in The Square, as well as some of the very few remaining thatched cottages.

To the north of The Square, Whittall Street (formerly High Street) and Red Lion Street run downhill to Richmond Street and Wales Street respectively. There is a great mixture of architectural styles but many houses are built of the ironstone which was quarried locally until the 1920s. Many were rebuilt after the disastrous fire of 1785 which destroyed 40 houses and caused damage amounting to £3,287.16s.5d. Several houses still bear the badges of the companies with whom the inhabitants insured.

Follow the 'Railway Station only' sign in the area known as Spinney Bank and again you will find a wonderful mixture of architecture, including the oldest cottage in the village, 'Q' cottage.

In 1664 the spring at Astrop was 'discovered' by two doctors, Richard Lower and Thomas Willis, who recommended their patients to take the waters at St Rumbold's Well rather than travel to Tonbridge. The next hundred years was a time of fame and prosperity. According to a pamphlet published in 1668, the waters were beneficial to 'all kinds of general disorders of the stomach, liver, spleen, kidneys, heart, brain, nerves and muscles'. A new well, the Bog Spring, was opened in 1749 but by 1777 Bray says 'the place is now out of fashion, the lodging houses are miserable', and Leamington Spa had become 'the' place to take the waters.

Lacemaking was an occupation of many women in the village in the 19th

The church of St Peter and St Paul at Kings Sutton

century and girls would attend the lacemaking school behind the stores in The Square rather than the general school in Astrop Road. The latter is now a private dwelling but still called The Olde School House.

⌘ LILBOURNE

The village of Lilbourne in the north-west of the country could easily be missed by travellers speeding along the A5, as it lies back from that part of the road known for the masts of Rugby Radio Station. It is a little rural oasis, closely bordered by Warwickshire and Leicestershire.

There is very little documentary evidence to piece together Lilbourne's history. It is not far from the Roman site called Tripontium. Many tantalizing archaeological sites abound, including a windmill and a watermill. The remains of two mottes and a bailey close to the river Avon make an impressive and unexpected sight from the motorway. Closer to the castle mounds lies All Saints' church, whose earliest construction goes back to the 13th and 14th centuries, although in recent years two Saxon doorways have been discovered. The Squat tower is balanced by the huge chestnut tree growing by the gate. Now the church, the Victorian rectory and Glebe Farm are all that remain of the former village, which became relocated on the hilltop.

In medieval times the proximity to the Watling Street and its merchants and sheep trade made Lilbourne a wealthy village. There was a market larger than the

Motte and bailey remains at Lilbourne

one at Rugby in the field now known as the Butts, and cobbles still remain in the yard of Glebe Farm.

⌘ LOIS WEEDON & WESTON BY WEEDON

The small hamlets of Lois Weedon and Weston by Weedon nestle in the south-west corner of Northamptonshire. The two hamlets combine to make a single community, with Weston claiming the pub and Lois Weedon the church, and the school conveniently placed halfway between the two.

In the 11th century Gilo de Pinkney built a castle in Wedone and the village became known as 'Weedon Pinkney'. All that remains of it today is a tree-covered mound beside the village green, which is greatly reduced from its original size.

The 11th century priory has also vanished and all that is left are the monks' fishponds in the field known as 'Church Close'. When the monks discovered a mineral spring to the south of the church they made it into a well and dedicated it to Saint Lucien. It became known as St Loys' well – this was the beginning of the village being known as Weedon St Loys. The water from the well was believed to have healing properties and it attracted many pilgrims.

The peaceful church, dedicated to St Mary and St Peter, witnessed a violent scene on Sunday, 2nd July 1643, when twelve Parliamentary troopers rode from Northampton to arrest the Anglican priest, William Losse.

Lois Weedon's peaceful church

There is a very weathered tombstone in the churchyard showing a woman handing a cup to her husband, which is supposed to contain poison. It is linked with the story about a woman who poisoned her husband and was burnt at the stake in a field near Weston. She was supposed to have been the last person to die at the stake in England.

Weston takes pride in possessing one of the oldest Baptist chapels in Northamptonshire, which was built in 1791. Until then baptisms took place in an open air baptistry at Cathanger Farm, near Woodend.

Until his death in 1988, Sir Sacheverell Sitwell, the youngest brother of Sir Osbert and Dame Edith Sitwell, lived at Weston Hall. Sir Sacheverell is buried beside his wife and his mother Lady Ida Sitwell in the churchyard extension. Dame Edith is also buried there, her grave marked by a tapering stone pillar on which is fixed a bronze plaque, by Henry Moore, depicting two delicate hands, the hands of Youth and Age.

Why the village is called 'Lois Weedon', when all the modern maps and signpost record it as 'Weedon Lois' remains a mystery. To many of the locals, in fact, it is still called by its ancient name of 'Loys Weedon'.

⌘ LONG BUCKBY

Long Buckby is certainly long, it stretches for one and a half miles, and has done so since the time of Elizabeth I when the prefix was first recorded. Historically it was

The Peacock at Long Buckby

an open village, independent, adaptable and radical. Now it contains several modern housing estates, which do not destroy the original character. It is mostly a dormitory village, with many amenities including a modern library.

Behind some Victorian terraced houses stand the 'shops' where the hand-sewn shoemakers formerly worked. The village was well known in the 19th and early 20th centuries for these shoemakers, who gained a considerable reputation. There were once several shoe factories, the largest of which had a world-wide reputation for riding boots and supplied the Royal Horse Guards.

The castle, which now comprises an oval ringwork surrounded by a ditch, is undocumented but may have been built by the de Quincy family, later the Earls of Winchester, who held the manor from the mid 12th to the mid 13th century.

The parish church is dedicated to St Lawrence, the tower dating back to the 12th century. The main part of the church was added later with subsequent alterations to the north and south aisles.

Nonconformity has been a very strong feature of this village. The United Reformed church was formally constituted in 1707 as the Independent chapel and the present building was erected in 1771. The Baptist church on the Market Place was founded in 1759 with the present church being built in 1846.

A very noticeable feature of the village is the variety of the forms of transport that pass through the parish, including the Roman Watling Street (now the A5) which forms the western boundary of the parish. In 1790 the Grand Junction Canal (now the Grand Union) was built at Buckby Wharf, linking London and Birmingham, and in 1830 the main railway line from Euston to Rugby passed within yards of the canal. The railway line near Northampton which provides Long Buckby with its station, one of only six in the county, was not built until 1880. Then in 1959 the M1 motorway was built near the canal and the railway. These features have in their time had some effect on life in Long Buckby.

⌘ LUDDINGTON-IN-THE-BROOK

The village, never large, developed as labourers' dwellings in meadows on both sides of the brook, until the landlord, the Duke of Buccleuch and Queensberry, had new cottages built beside the Hemington-Gidding road, above flood levels, in 1863. It is rarely named on maps and road atlases.

With equal rarity, a red VR letterbox is let into the wall of a small red brick former bakehouse at the end of a terrace of cottages that had been moved up from the river meadows. The 14th century church tops a low grassy knoll close to the brook, but sufficiently high to escape the frequent floods before the extensive land drainage of recent years.

At its eastern, Gidding, end, an enlarged cottage, once an off-licensed house, is some 200 yards within the Northants county boundary with Cambridgeshire, yet the village has no nameboard of identity. It's a place drivers often come upon by surprise, wondering just where they are and starting to look around as they're pulling away from it again!

Those who must have the blessings of urban life do not choose to live at Luddington. Folk here appreciate Nature in all its forms and moods. Officially classified as 'Open Country', no new building is allowed other than adaptations or extensions, at any rate up to the next County Structure Plan Review from the year 2001.

⌘ MAIDFORD

This is a small village with a very long history. Surrounded by lovely country and still a few woods, it is within easy reach of centres such as Daventry and Towcester. Inevitably the lifestyle of the place has changed considerably. It was formerly largely agricultural, and practically self-sufficient with a post office, general shop, blacksmith, carpenter cum undertaker, shoemaker, tailor and dressmaker etc, but today it is a commuter village, busy with traffic only at the beginning and end of the day.

In much earlier times it had a silk stocking industry employing many people. Pillow lace was also made and sold to help the family income. In the 1850s Leopold Stanton, a lace-designer, lived at The Villas, now Brook House. His lace designs were exhibited in many parts of the world. The gate to the driveway of his home, made by the village carpenter, was from his own design based on a Maltese

A peaceful scene at Maidford

lace pattern, and it became known as 'The Old Lace Gate'. Sadly it no longer exists, but in the driveway at the rear of the house remains can be seen of the same pattern laid out in bricks in the ground.

The church dedicated to St Peter and St Paul has a fine saddle-back tower and a very long history, the first rector being appointed in 1219. The manor house, now known as 'Manor Farm', adjacent to the church is thought to have been a monastery connected with the Augustinian priory at Canons Ashby.

Several springs in the area are impregnated with iron and mineral salt, and water from the chalybeate spring in the village was used for curing eye infections.

The peace and serenity of Maidford must have suited Elizabeth Wilson, for it is recorded that she died here in May 1767 at the extraordinary age of 122 years!

⌘ MARSTON ST LAWRENCE

Marston St Lawrence lies in the rolling countryside of south Northamptonshire, approximately halfway between Brackley and Banbury. Findings in and around the village suggest that a community existed here as far back as the 5th century and there are sites of interest relating to Roman times. Mention is made of 'Merestone' in the Domesday survey. The church of St Lawrence dates from the 11th century and has a Jacobean carved screen, separating the Lady Chapel from the north aisle. A yew tree, certified to be over a thousand years old, can be seen standing stout and strong outside the north door of the church.

Marston House and its lake

Situated nearby is Marston House, once the home of the Blencowe family whose roots dated back to 1446. Much evidence of this family can be seen on the memorials placed in the church, along with the hatchments displayed high on the wall at the west end of the church.

Within the grounds of Marston House is a lake surrounded by lawns and shrubbery, with a bridge dated 1759 over its south end. This provides an enjoyable walk around the edge of this attractive village.

⌘ MIDDLETON CHENEY

Middleton Cheney lies about three miles from Banbury, and approximately six miles west of Brackley on the A422. It has a long history and derives the second half of its name from the Chenduit family who were the Norman lords of Middleton at the time of the Domesday Book in 1086. Many of the older houses have historic associations such as tanning, glove-making, clockmaking, baking and hosiery weaving.

One of the first battles of the Civil War was fought at Middleton Cheney in May 1643; the site is now the Moors Drive housing estate. After the defeat of the Parliamentary forces, 46 of the Parliamentary soldiers were buried in the churchyard.

The 14th century church, built in the Decorated style, has a tower with six bells and a spire which rises to 150 ft. The church porch is of an unusual construction and only two other similar ones are known of, at Chacombe and Corby, the roof being made of stone sloping at an acute angle.

The church contains some of the best Edward Burne-Jones and William Morris stained glass in the country. Two windows in the chancel were created by Edward Burne-Jones as a memorial to his friend the Reverend William A. Buckley, who was a rector of Middleton Cheney from 1853 to 1892. The church was restored in 1865 under the direction of Sir Gilbert Scott. The church register dates from 1558.

⌘ MOULTON

Lying just north of the county town and surrounded by new estates, both residential and industrial, Moulton could easily have become a suburb of Northampton. However, this ancient village – mentioned in the Domesday Book as Moltone, but with a history that goes back to Roman times and even earlier – retains its individuality. The heart of the village, now a conservation area, remains essentially rural.

The parish church, dedicated to St Peter and St Paul, dates mostly from the late 13th century but Saxon remains, including the shaft of a cross, have been found nearby which shows that the site has been used for Christian worship since very early times.

A Methodist Society was formed in 1801. The present Methodist chapel was built in 1835 and has twice been enlarged over the years. Perhaps, however, the most widely known place of worship in Moulton is the Baptist church dating from the mid 17th century. Visitors come to see where the great William Carey was pastor, whose vision led to the formation of the Baptist Missionary Society in 1792.

Agriculture continues to play an important role in the life of the village. It is home to the Northamptonshire College of Agriculture, which developed from a Farm School opened in 1913.

On examining the information given in the early censuses (1841 and 1851) it appears that there were many tradesmen living in the area – the usual bakers and butchers, but also stonemasons, cordwainers (allied to the shoe trade), engineers and what are described as 'sojourners' (sometimes travelling tradesmen). There were, of course, the agricultural workers employed on the many farms and most of the women and girls were lacemakers. This was a thriving cottage industry.

It is thought that the old church room, built as a warehouse for the Co-op, became a pinafore factory attached to the Brook Company of Northampton – an early example of the spread of industry to villages around the town. In the latter part of the 19th century when the shoe factories were opened in Northampton many Moulton men (and women) walked to and from work in the shoe factories in the town.

One family well known in the village is the Jeyes family, members of which were Philadelphus Jeyes, chemist, and his brother John who invented the famous disinfectant Jeyes Fluid, as well as many other products.

⌘ Naseby

Naseby lies three miles east of Welford, not far from the county border. At 600 ft Naseby can be snowbound in winter, and daffodils take two weeks longer to appear here than in Market Harborough, the nearest town seven miles away. The village stands on the watershed of the Midlands, and among several water sources gives rise to both the 'Warwickshire' Avon which flows west and the northern tributary of the river Nene flowing to the east coast.

The pattern of village streets is very similar to that on the oldest recorded map of 1630 – Church Street and High Street running parallel and nearly north to south, Newlands across the top, Nutcote at the bottom, and School Lane and Gynwell in between – Gynwell named after a cleric of the Middle Ages.

The famous battle of 1645 was fought between King Charles I and the Parliamentarians with Sir Thomas Fairfax as Commander-in-Chief and Oliver Cromwell, at that stage, as Lieutenant-General of the Horse. The Parliamentarians carried the day following Cromwell's decisive charge. The battle was not recorded in the parish register but there are two monuments in the parish.

One of Naseby's monuments

One, erected in the 19th century on the site of an old windmill to the right of the road to Market Harborough, warns of the dangers to peoples who rise against their king. The other was put up in 1936 on the way to Sibbertoft and marks the spot from which Cromwell led his cavalry.

Inside the church of All Saints is the Cromwell Table, reputed to have been in the pub opposite (now Shuckborough House) on the eve of the battle, when advance troops of the King surprised Roundheads at rest and recreation. As usual, Cromwell is supposed to have stabled horses in the church. There is a Norman font, a very old brass of a man and his wife (though he has lost his head), and an enormous copper ball said to be loot from Boulogne in France, in 1544. It used to grace the 'stump' on the tower before the spire was built.

⌘ NASSINGTON

There has been a village settlement here since ancient times. An important archaeological discovery was made in 1942, during the reopening of an old gravel pit. A mechanical scraper, removing the topsoil, uncovered parts of an old Anglo-Saxon cemetery. About 50 graves were found, with quite valuable grave goods such as spear heads, shield bosses, bronze drinking cups and jewellery. Some were taken by Oundle School, but some examples are in Peterborough Museum.

The cemetery was rather near the river, and liable to flooding, so the settlement must gradually have moved higher up the hill, where the first Anglo-Saxon church was built, and around which the present village still clusters.

The prebendal manor house, 1230, is the oldest inhabited house in Northamptonshire, and stands over much of the old Anglo-Saxon site.

Excavations of parts of the gardens prove this. From these works it has been deduced that King Canute owned a royal manor here. It would have been a large wooden building with a single aisled timbered great hall. Some of the post holes of the foundations have been uncovered, determining its size. Near this settlement site an old stone quarry has been excavated, from which the first church was built.

⌘ NETHER HEYFORD

Heyford, or according to the Domesday Book, 'Heiforde', is situated to the west of Northampton in the valley of the river Nene and bordered by the Grand Union Canal. Since the 1960s the village has expanded rapidly due to better roads and the proximity of the M1 motorway.

The feature which strikes the eye as soon as one enters Heyford is the beautiful, tree-lined, five acre village green – certainly the most handsome for miles around. At one time cows and geese grazed there and washing was hung out to dry; it has also seen many keenly fought cricket and football matches. But with the new playing field, the green has reverted to its role of Heyford's 'lung'.

Perhaps the most famous (or infamous) character of the past was Francis Morgan, Judge of the King's Bench, who was said to have pronounced sentence of death on Lady Jane Grey and who then in 1558, full of remorse, took his own life with the lament 'Take away the Lady Jane from me'. His monument appears on the south wall of the church, showing him kneeling at an altar tomb with his wife and with their sons and daughters behind them.

The tree-lined village green at Nether Heyford

⌘ NEWTON BROMSWOLD

Newton Bromswold is one of the smallest villages in Northamptonshire, and is situated on the Bedfordshire border three miles south-east of the town of Rushden. The name of the village is derived from the fact that in Anglo-Saxon times the village was a new town in the Brunswald Forest.

Needham Langhorne owned the manor in 1644. One of his children, Mary, married a Robert Townsend and before emigrating to America the couple had their daughter, Mary, baptised at the church on the 15th July, 1669. Mary Townsend junior later married Captain John Washington of Virginia, who is known to have acted as guardian to Augustine Washington, the father of George, the first American president. The only remaining trace of the Langhorne family today in the village is a silver alms dish given by Needham Langhorne's second wife Barbara on her marriage in 1656.

The church, completed in 1272, is a small building of the Early English period and dedicated to St Peter. One of its more notable features is the medieval stained glass. A window in the north aisle shows the head of Hugh of Lincoln on a rare blue flower patterned background, and the only other glass like this in the Midlands is in All Souls College Chapel in Oxford. The churchyard still retains the base for the old village cross.

Electricity was installed in the village in 1951 and with it came the disposal of a large quantity of oil lamps into the nearest pond! They may be collectable now, and some villagers may regret throwing them out, but back in 1951 Newton was glad to have 'the electric'.

⌘ NORTON

The pretty, mostly stone-built village of Norton lies two miles east of Daventry on a site it has inhabited since prehistoric times. It is mentioned in the Domesday Book.

Norton Hall was inhabited by the Knightley family of Fawsley in the reign of Elizabeth I. The marble tomb of Lady Elizabeth Seymour, second wife of Sir Richard Knightley, is situated in the beautiful 13/14th century church. She was the daughter of the Duke of Somerset, Lord Protector of England, in the reign of Edward VI.

Before 1840, the village used to surround the church but local legend has it that Beriah Botfield, the then owner of Norton Hall, had the village demolished and moved because he had a lady friend who used to visit him whom he did not want observed by the gossiping villagers! One row of cottages is known as Tattle Bank Row as the local women used to chat over the wall during the day.

Sadly in 1947 Norton Hall was blown up by the British Army as there was no one prepared to restore this splendid old building. All that remain are the coach-houses, blacksmith's shop, stables and the ice house.

Stone-built houses at Norton

⌘ ORLINGBURY

The village of Orlingbury lies within the triangle of main roads linking the nearby towns of Kettering, Northampton and Wellingborough and so it still has much of its rural character without major developments and heavy traffic. Orlingbury Hundred, the ancient grouping which comprised fifteen parishes in the rural area between these towns, derived its name from this parish in recognition of the earlier importance of this community which contained two manors with all their associated feudal history.

The village green remains the heart of Orlingbury, and the focal point for much of the everyday village activity. Clustered around it is a medley of buildings old and new, including several traditional ones constructed in the local stone, often with ironstone used for the decorative masonry. These include the former forge and school with adjoining schoolmaster's house which was built in 1845. The three major listed buildings of the village – Orlingbury Hall, The Old Rectory and the parish church – are all around the edge of the green.

Dominating the scene is the church whose square tower is a landmark visible from far afield. Older residents of Orlingbury still recall with a chuckle that whilst they were told, as children going out to play, not to get out of sight of the church – they knew that this still gave them plenty of scope to wander. The parish church of St Mary was completely rebuilt in 1842 to a new design by the architect R. H. Hussey. It stands on the same site as the former church which had fallen into decay and was deemed to be a grave danger to all who entered it. The style of the present church is that of the early Victorian Gothic revival such that the church is often thought by visitors to be far older than it actually is.

Orlingbury Hall occupies the site of the former manor house which was lived in successively by the Lanes, Toftes and Chybnalles. In 1678 this contained twenty rooms and paid taxes on twenty hearths but was replaced early in the 18th century by the present Hall, built by Richard Young whose family held the manor for the next two centuries. The Dower House can be seen across the road to the west of the Hall, opposite a gate in the wall which served as a short link between the lord of the manor and his widowed mother.

Other buildings which have survived from this time include the Dovecote opposite to the entrance of The Old Rectory, and various farmhouses and cottages which have now all been modernised internally. There remain numerous wells, from which the village derived its water in days of old, and several residents remember times before the arrival of modern amenities such as electricity and mains drainage. Today's villagers face the future with the assurance that many of the best aspects of village life have been retained for enjoyment by all, both those who grew up within sight of the Orlingbury church tower and those who came from farther afield to settle and make Orlingbury their home.

⌘ PASSENHAM

Passenham is a hamlet consisting of about a dozen houses, and the church of St Guthlac. There is also a mill, a manor house and a tithe barn dating from 1500.

A church was first mentioned in AD 921, but the present one is 13th to 14th century. The chancel was beautified by Sir Robert Bannister in the 1620s. In recent years a unique set of murals have been uncovered in the chancel, part of Sir Robert Bannister's great scheme of prophets and evangelists, dated 1628.

Many ghost stories are connected with Passenham. A Deanshanger girl leaped into the mill stream one night and was crushed by the mill wheel, and some time later, at midnight on Deanshanger Feast, a scream was heard from the stream. The verger told a tale of how, one stormy night while ringing the bell, his candle blew out. He let go of the rope to light it again, but the bell kept ringing! Then there is the phosphorescent skeletal form of a huntsman with a broken neck, dragged in the stirrups of a phantom steed, which disappears among the gravestones. This one is known as Bobby Bannister's Ghost, after a man who was killed in a riding accident.

⌘ PATTISHALL

Pattishall and its neighbouring villages are set in a rural area on the borders of the Northamptonshire Heights and the Nene valley. The parish lies four miles

'2000 years of history' in Pattishall, Astcote, Eastcote and Dalscote are celebrated on this sign

north of Towcester on the Roman Watling Street. It comprises the villages of Pattishall, Astcote, Eastcote, Dalescote and Foster's Booth.

Pattishall, the largest village in the parish, is mentioned in the Domesday Book. The church of Holy Cross stands on a small limestone plateau and dates from Saxon times. Although a lot of the village has been developed in recent years, there are many attractive old stone houses in the narrow street which leads to the village green.

The village of Astcote had a thriving industry well over a hundred years ago. There were at one time three small factories involved with shoe-making. The raw materials were collected from Northampton and turned into handmade shoes and boots, often in the cottages. Many of the present day villagers have ancestors who were involved in the shoe trade, and the same family names have remained in the village.

Eastcote is still basically a farming village, although the cows no longer walk down the main street on their way to be milked. Eastcote does have a small claim to fame, being mentioned in *The Times* on the 5th January 1915. During the First World War, an internment camp was established here for German seamen. One of the inhabitants wrote a letter which was published in the newspaper, about life in the camp. He stated: 'The natives of our village are very nice. They bring us cigarettes, fruit and papers and stop to chat.' Many of the prisoners whiled away the time making model boats, and a complete model harbour was built by the brook.

Dalscote, now a small hamlet, was once the site of a larger settlement. In the surrounding fields overlooking Northampton, stone rubble and post-medieval pottery have been found. Where once there was habitation, there are now crops on the rolling landscape.

The name Foster's Booth derives from Forester's Booth, and the present Peggotty's Restaurant used to be that inn. There is some decorative raised plaster-work on the south side on the building of a hunting scene. The ancient royal forests of Whittlewood used to lie to the south and the hunters could well have visited Foster's Booth to partake of refreshments.

⌘ POLEBROOK

The village of Polebrook, three miles to the south-east of Oundle, contains within its parish boundaries two other settlements, Armston and Kingsthorpe, and clearly derives the second part of its name from the brook which flows into the river Nene about three quarters of a mile to the west of the village. The thriving community enjoys the obvious beauty of this village with its many old houses, mainly built in local stone with roofs of thatch, Collyweston slates and tiles.

Its most beautiful building, dominating the centre of the village, is the church of All Saints. Mainly Early English, with some Norman work remaining, both the exterior and interior are characterised by an impressive simplicity. Polebrook's most eminent rector must have been Dr John Wilkins, brother-in-law of Oliver Cromwell and a founder-member of the Royal Society.

A Roll of Honour in the church lists the many American servicemen of the 351st Bombardment Group who were killed while flying from Polebrook airbase during the Second World War. A memorial has also been erected on the site of the former airfield at the end of what was the main runway. It was at this base (whatever the claims of other places!) that Clark Gable served.

In the 'Square' in the village centre is clustered a particularly attractive collection of stone cottages, the Old Duke's Head, formerly a public house, forming one side of the group. Behind a small green near the war memorial stands another fine stone house with a painted tiled roof and it was from this building, when – many years ago – it was a post office, that the first old age pensions, 'Lloyd George's ten shillings', were issued. Later, the post office moved to another well-set 18th century house, the Gables, in the main street. Its final destination, before the village became stampless, was in the converted Wesleyan chapel nearly opposite the school. This, and the school were the only Victorian buildings of any significance. One of the oldest houses, beyond the school, on the way out to Lutton, is the Manor, dating at least to the 16th century. Undoubtedly the grandest house, imposing behind its wrought iron gates in the main street, is Polebrook Hall.

⌘ POTTERSPURY

The village was originally called Pyrie or Estpirie (East Perey), derived from 'pyrige' meaning 'the place where pear trees grow'. Following the introduction of potteries in the 12th century the name was changed to Potters Perry or Potterspury. Several of these ancient potteries have been excavated in recent years.

The parish church is dedicated to St Nicholas and there has been a church on the site since at least 1087.

An Independent church was established in 1690 by the Rev Michael Harrison. The history of the Independents in the 18th century is largely bound up with the name John Heywood. He was an eccentric and remarkable man, described as tall and thin with a mean and slovenly appearance, mostly due to the neglect of his imprudent wife who remained outside the church for the first 28 years of their unsuitable marriage. However, he was held in high esteem by many including the Duke of Grafton, who allowed him to use his library.

The Dukes of Grafton resided at Wakefield Lodge from about 1748, when the 2nd Duke commissioned William Kent to design and build a house on the site of a hunting lodge in the Whittlebury Forest, about a mile south of Potterspury. Kent brought in Capability Brown to landscape the park. Following the death of the 7th Duke in 1918 the estate was broken up and sold.

Within and close to the village were several farms which employed most of the men before the advent of the railways and their workshops at Wolverton. Many of the women and girls were employed in lacemaking. The census return for 1851 lists 135 lacemakers, some of whom were as young as five.

A brook runs through the village and at one time supplied power to a corn and grinding mill. This power was later supplemented by a steam engine and later still by an oil engine. The mill continued in use until the 1940s.

⌘ PRESTON CAPES

Preston Capes stands amidst the Northamptonshire Heights in delightful countryside six miles from Daventry. The main street rises steeply to reach 594 ft above sea level. The village, once known as Preston Magna, formed part of the Fawsley estate until 1932 when most of the properties were offered for sale. At that time the majority had thatched roofs. Included in the parish is the hamlet of Little Preston, once known as Preston Parva, about half a mile away towards Maidford.

William the Conqueror awarded the area to a French knight, Hugh de Capes (Hughes Capet), after 1066. He built a castle on the site of the Roman encampment, which is now occupied by the manor house. Traces of the castle walls can still be found there. Behind the row of houses and bungalows in Church Way there is believed to be a Saxon ditch in which a Saxon ring was found and nearby a Saxon axe.

The deer park at Preston Capes

After the manor house the next most important house is the School House, which was built around 1690. The most unusual properties are Archway Cottages, which were built in the 18th century as four cottages (now two) for workers from Fawsley House. They have a red brick connecting archway which when viewed from Fawsley Park looks like a castle.

The old school, near the church, was built in 1845, enlarged in 1871 and closed in 1965. Part of the old rectory, next to the church, dates from the 16th century and is built on the site of a priory founded in 1090. The church of St Peter and St Paul dates from the beginning of the 13th century, with periodic improvements and additions.

⌘ PYTCHLEY

The lords of the manor of Pytchley in the 11th century owed a service to the King, as did many other landowners. Their particular service was to maintain hunting dogs with which to kill wolves and foxes in Northants and the surrounding counties. The 'service' was maintained until the reign of Charles II in the 17th century. It was common knowledge that Pytchley had been noted for its hunting packs 'before the Conquest'.

Pytchley's comparative closeness to London led to many of the hunting gentry buying or renting mansions here for hunting over the centuries. The Isham family held lands in Pytchley from the 14th century and in 1580 Sir Euseby Isham built the

Hall, a large elegant mansion facing west to the church, sited across the present Isham Road.

Other rich families lived in the Hall and in the mid 18th century the famous pack of hounds was formally founded. It was maintained at the Hall until 1824, when due to the gambling debts of the owner George Payne, the Hall had to be demolished. The kennels moved permanently to Brixworth.

Pytchley church dates from Norman times and has been added to through the centuries. The large size of the church reflects the greater numbers living in Pytchley when the Hall and other large mansions and farms required huge staffs.

Villagers through the centuries, if not connected in some way with the Hunt, carved a living from agriculture. The village was largely self-supporting, with certain families tending to be blacksmiths, bakers, butchers, cobblers and carriers. In 1607 there were 'disorders' when the violent-tempered Sir Euseby carried out certain land enclosures, but other crimes in the village tended to be only on a petty scale.

When the Hall was demolished, much employment was lost. The 1851 census shows a new way of literally getting 'pin-money' – 63 lacemakers among the villagers, making coarse lace to famous Flemish and Belgian designs. The later machine-lace of Nottingham would kill this trade.

In the late 19th century the population was surprisingly large. In 1898 the Midland Railway Company was building the line from Kettering, and labourers and their families lived in Pytchley. A great rivalry existed between the families running the two chapels – the Methodists led by the shopkeeper Sewell family, and the Wesleyans led by the coal merchant Woolleys. Village children benefited from the rival events on successive nights organised by the chapels – and by the church!

⌘ RINGSTEAD

Ringstead parish is located between Thrapston and Raunds, in East Northamptonshire. The name may be derived from one of the ancient parish fields, the Anglo Saxon 'hring' meaning a circular place. The village was first documented in 1124. We are in footwear country, and shoemaking was formerly carried out in the village hall and elsewhere.

Ringstead's oldest building is the mainly 13th century church of St Mary, in the Early English style with some Decorated portions. The Baptists have had a chapel in the village since 1714, although the present one was erected in 1785. In addition, there is a Methodist chapel (from 1857) on the site of the former blacksmith's shop.

There are also many private residences in the parish that have been built from the attractive local ironstone, in differing shades of brown, usually alternated with the lighter freestone; most of these date from the 17th and 18th centuries.

Lower Ringstead Lock

Ringstead was the birthplace of Alf Roberts, father of Margaret Thatcher. Many generations of her ancestors, humble shoemakers and labourers, lived in Ringstead.

⌘ ROTHERSTHORPE

Rothersthorpe is an old, old village full of secrets. Situated on the prehistoric Jurassic Way, it has at its heart an ancient earthworks – The Berry.

Here the future Northamptonshire may have been born when in AD 918 the Saxon army of Edward the Elder, marching on Northampton from its base at Towcester, defeated the Danish forces to the south-west of the town, and annexed the area covered by the present day county. The post-enclosure (1810) farm of Danesfield could represent the approximate site of this encounter.

The village church of St Peter and St Paul again has very ancient origins. Little is known beyond the present building, which owes much to the monks of St James' Abbey, Northampton. Older edifices must have stood on the site of the church, to which the base of a 7th century preaching cross and a Norman font bear eloquent witness.

⌘ RUSHTON

The ancient, scattered but neat, village of Rushton, was mentioned in the Domesday Book as Riston or Risetone.

Many 17th century buildings remain, although now changed to residential occupation. They are built mainly of the buff coloured oolite ironstone found locally and in more recent years quarried for the steelworks at nearby Corby. A good example of this pleasant mellowed stonework can be seen in the buildings constituting the High Street post office and general stores, with its stable, bakehouse and upper level granary still there, but adapted for present day use.

In High Street is the village pub, the Thornhill Arms, named after an early lord of the manor, and there is an excellent view of the parish church of All Saints, with the cricket field and pavilion just below. The north chapel (chantry) of All Saints was used for many years as the village school, with the school-master remunerated in earlier times by the patronage of the lord of the manor residing at Rushton Hall.

Just beyond the junction of High Street and Manor Road stands the old forge which was used until just after the Second World War. The older part is now a workshop and garage for a modern residence, built on the site of the blacksmith's yard.

The Triangular Lodge ot Rushton

Rushton Hall has historical connections with the Tresham family – Thomas Tresham, the builder, being the grandson of Sir Thomas Tresham, the last Lord Prior (in England) of the Knights Hospitallers of St John of Jerusalem. Francis Tresham was involved in the conspiracy leading to the ill-fated Gunpowder Plot, and relied on his uncle, Thomas the builder, for funds.

Another of Tresham's buildings, well chronicled, is the Triangular Lodge, built on the north-west perimeter of the Hall grounds. It is easily reached by following the road to Desborough. During springtime, the hall grounds are carpeted with snowdrops and in days past these were sent to London from Rushton station.

⌘ SCALDWELL

The village lies just off the A508 Northampton to Market Harborough road, behind Brixworth. Its green is surrounded by many trees and the 12th century church stands on a hillside behind it, with its beautiful, pinnacled sanctus bell tower.

In the churchyard are the remains of a preaching cross and legend has it that somewhere in the village is hidden the stained glass from the church windows, taken to save it from the Roundheads – but, unfortunately, never found.

There was once a healing well in the village and at least 20 other wells scattered around, became the name Scaldwell actually means 'shallow welling out of water'. The pond on the green was the original source of water for the village pump. This in turn fed a series of horse troughs, all of which have been buried – leaving only the blue brick pump housing exposed. The Town 'Well' House is the oldest in the village and at the time of the Dissolution of the Monasteries under Henry VIII, several people were arrested here for trying to conceal church plate and relics. The 'Town Well' charity remains to this day.

The artist George Clark – famous in print circles for his pictures of important houses – lived in the village and the author H. E. Bates stayed here on several occasions. He reputedly used Scaldwell as the setting for his novel *Love for Lydia*.

Like most small villages it supported its own mill – operational until 1916 – but unusually there was also a 'vellum factory' run by two eccentric brothers.

Up until the 1950s ironstone quarries were worked around Scaldwell and visitors would enter the village under the railway, reminiscent of a cable-car, carrying hanging buckets overhead. Now all that remains are the parapets of the bridges at the road sides. The railway has long gone, the tunnels filled and the ground levelled, so that anyone looking over the bridge would only see flat fields.

It is said that there was a 'Grey Lady', who walked the village heavily veiled. This was reputedly the ghost of Madeleine Bell, a Scottish murderess whose case was found 'Not Proven' under Scottish law for the murder of her fiancé. There are several other reported ghosts in Scaldwell – but all friendly. They include a whistling groom and mysterious flames seen flickering inside a house.

⌘ SIBBERTOFT

Outwardly Sibbertoft has changed little over the years. It sits on top of the hills near the boundary of Leicestershire and Northamptonshire. Being over 600 ft above sea level, in winter, snow often covers the village when the valleys below are quite clear. The surrounding rolling countryside is typical of the hunting Shires and the famous Pytchley Hunt meets in the village each year.

The river Welland rises in the village, in the cellar of the old rectory. It emerges north of the village and over the centuries has formed the lovely Welland valley. It finally reaches the North Sea at the Wash.

The church, dedicated to St Helen, records rectors back to 1220, but is certainly much older. Clerics have included the Rev Miles Berkeley, a 19th century botanist. He published several reference books and 'made notable discoveries regarding Vine Disease Fungi'. There was also James Sturgis, the Hunting Curate who conducted services wearing riding clothes and boots under his robes. His family were the last to live in the Mansion House, which was at the bottom of Westhorpe Lane, then called Cattle End. The house had been knocked down by 1877, though why is not known.

The Civil War disturbed the peace of the area, especially in 1645 when the Battle of Naseby was fought nearby. Most of the fighting took place a few miles to the south, though King Charles' standard was raised at Moot Hill to the east of Sibbertoft. Coombe Hill saw both the King's army marching up to the battle and bands of wounded survivors escaping northwards after the battle was lost.

By the 1890s, much of the land belonged to the Villers family. The autocratic Lady Elizabeth Villers lived at Sulby Hall and ruled the villagers with a rod of iron. Riding to church each Sunday, if she saw washing hanging outside the home of any employee, the offending family was dismissed. In 1897 her will stipulated that her funeral carriage be pulled by matching black horses, to be shot after the funeral.

Her niece, Miss Elizabeth Mansell, inherited the land and Sulby Hall – sadly, knocked down in the 1950s for the lead on its roof. In 1911, she built the reading room in memory of her two brothers, both killed in the army. This memorial became an important amenity which has given much pleasure to the village ever since.

⌘ SILVERSTONE

The origins of Silverstone go a long way back into history: at one time it lay deep in the heart of the ancient Whittlewood Forest and its inhabitants made their living from charcoal-burning and other woodland crafts. The forest was rich in game and in the 12th century a royal hunting lodge was in use in the centre of the village by King John. Although the lodge is long gone, it was close to a series of fish-breeding ponds, the earthworks of which can still be seen to the west of a part of the village known as Little London. This is believed to be so called because refugees fleeing London at the time of the Black Death settled here.

But, as in most other parts of the country, the Black Death took its toll in and around Silverstone. A hamlet, Charlock, was decimated and abandoned; the remains of its field system, hollow-ways ponds and house-platforms are still clearly visible as earthworks on a hill to the west of the present village. Another victim of the plague was Luffield Abbey, once a thriving monastic community, where everyone perished. The abbey fell into ruins and the last traces were finally obliterated in the Second World War when an aerodrome was built over the site. This aerodrome was converted into the world-famous Silverstone Racing Circuit and the monastery is remembered in the naming of Abbey Curve on the race-track.

For most of the time the village is a peaceful, rural place and there are still remnants of Whittlewood Forest close by: Hazelborough Forest and Bucknell Wood, run by the Forestry Commission, are much used by local people.

Although it has no pretensions to being a 'picture-postcard' village, Silverstone does have many old, attractive and interesting buildings, some of them listed, and of course there are many tales of the ghosts which haunt them. For example, there is a mysterious phantom woman's face which appears in a local farmhouse's upper window, and even an old chap in a cloth cap and carpet slippers who announces his presence with the smell of stale tobacco smoke! Luffield Abbey is supposed to have been haunted by a deer with a strangely human face and there are stories of headless horsemen being seen at night on the Old Riding in West End and other parts of the village. Finally, the ghost of a mistress of King John is believed to appear in the Compasses, a previous village pub now a private house, where she is reputed to have been foully murdered one night. But not many local people will own up to having seen any of these apparitions!

⌘ SOUTHWICK

Southwick is three miles north of Oundle, and lies in a valley. On the slope to the north is a spur of Rockingham Forest, and to the south is Short Wood, a Northants Wildlife Trust property renowned for its bluebells.

When Southwick is approached via the Woodnewton road, the first thing to catch one's eye is the Hall, an interesting, rambling, hotch-potch of architectural styles dating from the 14th century. The house has only been owned by three different families and even they were connected. The Knyvetts from the 12th century to 1441, the Lynnes to the early 1800s, and the Caprons to the present day. There are many legends associated with the house, mainly from the Lynne occupation. Mary Queen of Scots' burial certificate is said to be walled up in the house.

The parish church, dedicated to St Mary the Virgin, is adjacent to the Hall.

The tranquil stream in the grounds of Southwick Hall

Originally built by the Knyvett family in about 1230 with the tower and spire added by Sir John Knyvett in about 1350, the church was extensively rebuilt by the Lynnes in the 18th century.

The local pub is the thatched Shuckburgh Arms, believed to be of 16th century origin. It was bought into the estate by Mr George Capron in about 1839 and was named after his cousin, the Rev J. Shuckburgh.

⌘ STOKE ALBANY

Stoke Albany has some of the best features of a Northamptonshire village. Around the tranquil beauty of the village green is set an old hall house, a medieval church, chestnut trees in the churchyard, the war memorial in front of them and meadows and cornfields on the hills beyond. The scene has hardly altered during the last 100 years, except the prunus trees on the green which were planted to commemorate the Queen's Coronation.

The village was mentioned in the Domesday Book, and in the 13th century William de Albini, lord of the manor, from whom the village takes its name, laid out a new settlement consisting of four parallel streets together with a new manor house.

There are many old original buildings, some lying in the four parallel streets off Ashley Road. The oldest building in Stoke Albany is the church. The manor house situated in Ashley Road is a lovely stone house with stone mullioned windows and leaded lights. Thanks to conservation little of the outside has changed.

The church is dedicated to St Botolph, a monk and patron saint of travellers. As a reminder of the days when tarmac paths and roads were not in evidence, over the porch is a wooden tablet requesting that men shall scrape their shoes and women take off their pattens before entering.

⌘ STOKE BRUERNE

In 1902 a young pupil at the village school wrote a description of her home – 'It is a very pretty village situated in South Northamptonshire with a population of 400. The Grand Junction Canal runs straight through the village, it is specially interesting because of its locks and the tunnel, the boats have to be taken through the tunnel by means of a steam tug which goes from 5 am in the morning till 9 pm at night every two hours. The Towcester and Olney Railway runs through the parish and has a station about half a mile from the village. The line is now only open for luggage as passengers did not pay.

'The chief occupations of the people are agricultural labourers and working in the Brick-field and on the Grand Junction Canal. We have a full post and telegraph office in the village, we have one delivery of letters and two going out posts. There is one public house, The Boat Inn. There is one blacksmith's shop and two shoemaker's shops and five grocer's shops. We have two woods in the parish, The Plain Wood and Stoke Park woods. The only drawback in Stoke Bruerne is that we are so very short of clear pure water in summer.'

Today, the biggest single employer is the Boat Inn, a free house, now extended beyond its bars to a tea room and a separate restaurant. Although the farms are much the same, fewer people are employed on them. British Waterways employs a

A bustling canal scene at Stoke Bruerne

number of people, some on maintenance of the canal, some in their Waterways Museum and several in their souvenir shop.

Much of the property once owned by the Duke of Grafton has been sold. Mains water and main drainage came to the village in the 1950s. The brickyard no longer produces bricks and the railway line has been scrapped and the land sold to the farmers whose land it ran through.

The village, situated between the greatly expanded Northampton and Milton Keynes and only four miles from the M1 is now within very easy reach of London.

⌘ STOWE IX CHURCHES

The hamlets of Church Stowe and Upper Stowe, together with half a dozen houses in between, combine to make the parish of Stowe IX Churches.

Not only is this community a happy one, it is a fortunate one, for the Stowes are set high, thus commanding views of a hilly landscape which seems to move as the light varies. No towering mountains here, no rocky outcrops, nothing dramatic, just a deeply satisfying and gentle beauty.

There are several theories as to how the name of Stowe IX Churches was derived. In medieval times the village was simply known as Stowe, meaning holy place. It was also known as Stowe-Ni-Churches at one time, and was perhaps changed by a clerical error. Some say that as Stowe is over 500 ft above sea level, nine churches could be seen. The ancient manor house stands next to the church, and it is possible that at one time the lord of the manor was the patron of nine parishes. An old legend tells of how the builders of the church unwittingly chose a site near to a fairy ring in the centre of England. Each time they started building, the fairies and goblins came at night and knocked down the stones. After the eighth attempt, a praying monk remained at the site throughout the night. This seemed to have been effective as at the ninth attempt the building was left standing and the workmen were able to complete their task.

⌘ SUDBOROUGH

Sudborough, nestling in a wooded hollow off the busy A6116 between Thrapston and Corby, still retains the olde worlde charm of earlier times.

The village is in the heart of the old Rockingham Forest, and there are still enough woods and new forests around to give it a secluded, private appearance. That is helped by the three roads into the village: the main entrance, off the A6116, features a severe bend forcing traffic to slow; the Newton Lane turning, further up the A6116 towards Corby, is a narrow, high-hedged road that looks particularly uninviting for traffic. And the other way in, the best, with a lovely aspect of the village from an overlooking hillside, is from Slipton, itself another sleepy village.

Most of the residents will tell you that Sudborough is the prettiest and nicest village in the county; regulars at the Vane Arms will swear it is the friendliest pub selling the best beer in Northamptonshire! Whatever the pub regulars say, and however much some may mourn the passing of the old village brewer, All Saints' church is the chief glory of the village. Its setting, near Harper's Brook, and its dignified, mellow stonework, add an aura of agelessness to the village.

A booklet available in the church chronicles its varied and chequered history, and much of the village itself. It includes details of the crusading de Veres, the occasion when the parish was closed illegally, the time when Highland troops were defeated and one was buried in a place later known as The Soldier's Grave, and the much-recounted tale of one parishioner, Samuel Mayes, who met a tragic end in a poaching affray. A song, handed down over the years and still sung at village events, begins:

> 'Poor Samuel Mayes of Sudborough Town,
> A lad of well-known fame,
> Who took delight both day and night,
> To hunt the lofty game.'

⌘ SULGRAVE

Sulgrave is a compact and attractive village located in a sparsely populated area of undulating and pleasant countryside and lies five miles north of Brackley, ten miles west of Towcester, and seven miles east of Banbury. The village marks a settlement of the early Britons, as discovered during archaeological excavations between 1960–80, on the site of the Saxon castle.

Sulgrave Manor

There are a number of important listed buildings in the village, in particular the 16th century Sulgrave Manor, ancestral home of the Washington family. Other important larger buildings include the Rectory Farm complex, the 18th century vicarage, the Thatched House Hotel and the Old Farmhouse.

The church of St James the Less was built in the 14th century although the base of the tower is Saxon. A tomb in the south aisle is the resting place of Lawrence Washington and his family, ancestors of George Washington, the first President of the United States of America. The four panels of Elizabethan glass above the Washington pew show the mullets and bars which may have inspired the stars and stripes.

Many visitors still come to Sulgrave throughout the year including a large number of Americans who come to view the ancestral home of their first president. Although much of the village has undoubtedly changed over the last 100 years the intrinsic charm still remains.

⌘ SYWELL

The centre of Sywell still retains its old world charm, with its small green surrounded by cottages, which outwardly have not changed since they were built in the mid 19th century by the Loyd family as a model village. Also on the green are the church and old school, now converted to a village hall.

Just off the green is Sywell Hall, a fine Elizabethan house. For a time the Tresham family, of Guy Fawkes fame, lived here. It is believed that Mary Queen of Scots stayed here, and while here mislaid a ring. When the house was being renovated at the beginning of the 20th century a ring was found, believed to have been that lost all those years ago.

Another family to live at the Hall were the Pells, who started a charity in the village. Watkin Owen Pell joined the navy at 11 years old and lost a leg in battle when he was 12 years old. Despite this he had a distinguished naval career, rising to the rank of admiral.

Sywell has rather an unusual ghost. The story is concerned with a great Turf scandal. In 1884 *Running Rum* won the Derby, but was challenged as being a four year old and not a three year old. During the ensuing law suit the horse could not be produced. 'You will never see the horse again,' the judge was told, 'but you may have a quarter of him if you like.' *Running Rum* was brought to Sywell at dead of night, butchered and buried in the grounds of Sywell House. People have told of hearing a phantom horse come up the yard and buckets rattling.

Many Second World War pilots remember Sywell as where they learnt to fly, often on a five week intensive course. This was not only British pilots but also those of the Free French Air Force. During the war Sywell was the centre for the repair of Wellington bombers. Planes or their parts were brought in on 'Queen Mary' lorries, to be put together and flown out to take part in the war again.

Besides having an industrial estate (utilising some of the wartime buildings) Sywell is known for its recreational facilities. Sywell Country Park, which includes the old Sywell reservoir, is a good example of nature conservation and provides opportunities for birdwatching and country walks.

⌘ TANSOR

Tansor is an ancient village and there has been a settlement here since pre-Roman times. The Domesday Book recorded the village as Tanesovre.

The church of St Mary dates in part from Saxon times and rectors are recorded by name since the 13th century. Of particular interest are the carved misericords, which include carvings of the falcon and fetterlock, an emblem of the House of York.

On 17th September 1819 a farmer called John Cave conveyed a portion of land to trustees, the rents to be used to relieve poverty in Tansor. It was to be used for 'clothing, meat, blankets, coal or other necessaries at the discretion of the rector and churchwardens on Christmas Day forever.' The land is still let for agricultural use, though the income is now used for wider charitable purposes.

The 19th century saw the advent of the railway, with a line running through Tansor from Peterborough to Northampton. However, the source of employment remained, the land, with the church as a focal point of village life. It was the coming of the motor car in the 20th century which started the decline of the village sense of community, here as elsewhere. Agriculture became mechanised and only a small number of people living in the village are involved now.

There are people still living in Tansor who have known two public houses in the

Tansor village

village, the White Horse and the Black Horse. Both, now, are private residences. There were two bakehouses, one at the rear of the Old Post Office, where bake ovens can still be seen. In the 19th century this baker kept the White Horse. Milling was carried out at the windmill, still standing but without sails or any other working parts. Another bakehouse stood against Elm House, also in Main Street. A blacksmith's forge was situated at the thatched cottage next to Greystones.

⌘ THORPE MANDEVILLE

The earliest mention of the parish is to be found in the Domesday Book, where it is styled Torp. The manor was held by the Pinkneys and was passed to the family of Amundville in about 1243, from whom the name Thorpe Mandeville comes.

From the churchyard can be seen the Ox-yard, which in the 13th century was the site of Thorpe Feast, usually taking place on the Sunday following the 6th July. A lofty avenue of elm trees at the western end of this wonderful field marked the area occupied by the original manor house.

The Ox-yard pond was a glorious meeting place for the children – for newt-catching in the summer, for finding pale autumn crocuses on the bank, for skating in the winter. There was a cricket pitch and green pavilion there, where teams from neighbouring villages came to play. Village children would swarm up the stone wall to play on the smooth grass at play time.

The manor house at Thorpe Mandeville

The old manor house was garrisoned by Oliver Cromwell in the Civil War and the mounds thrown up at this time were still visible in 1897 (as recorded by the Rev Algernon Guise Humphrey in the parish magazine). The 'new' manor house was built east of the church by Cromwell's niece.

The most ancient 'big house' in the village was the rectory – now the Court, which is about 400 years old and is a fine house with pastures for grazing. 'The Doctors Close' is so called because the Rev Nathaniel Humphrey's living was held by a Doctor Deacle who farmed this plot, and also kept his calves in the little field in the corner by Bulls Lane. It was called Calves Close.

The Three Conies has a sun dial on its wall with the dates 1622 and 1847 inscribed. The inn has certainly refreshed villagers for many a year and has also been a meeting place for the Bicester Hounds. There have been colourful gatherings both here and at the manor house. Before 1850 the magistrates held their meetings at the Three Conies.

Behind the pub was a garden called the saw-yard and a large stone house with substantial dovecote. This no longer remains, but a row of cottages called Dove Cottages and Dove Close are reminders of what once was. Ivy Cottage, another lovely old building, was the home of the shoemaker.

⌘ TITCHMARSH

The passer-by approaching Titchmarsh, especially from the Oundle-Thrapston

Titchmarsh's spectacular church tower

road, is soon aware of the village's outstanding feature, the square and pinnacled 15th century tower of the church of St Mary the Virgin, crowning the ridge on which the village stands.

Apart from its spectacular tower, the church has many interesting features, including the ha-ha which marks the churchyard boundary on west and south sides. There is a fine ring of eight bells, used regularly by the local team and visiting ringers from far and wide.

The domestic architecture of Titchmarsh ranges from 17th and 18th century cottages, some thatched, through to present-day barn conversions.

It is a village with historic connections; John Dryden, the 17th century Poet Laureate, spent his boyhood here, and in 1668 Samuel Pepys came to Titchmarsh for the marriage of his friend John Creed to 'Betty' Pickering, only daughter of Sir Gilbert and Lady Elizabeth Pickering. In the church there are fine memorials to members of the Pickering and Creed families, two painted by Elizabeth Creed, (née Pickering) at an advanced age.

⌘ WAPPENHAM

The ancient village of Wappenham at the heart of England is small and friendly and boasts few claims to fame. Many of the houses in the village are large and attractively built of Helmdon stone or red brick, but none so large as to suggest the presence of a resident squire at any time.

Back in the Middle Ages, Wappenham was a forest village subject to special laws and privileges and with direct connections to the king. It stood at the crossroads of England, with the Welsh Lane and Oxford Lane crossing at the top of the parish, Watling Street a few minutes ride away and important roads to Brackley, Buckingham and beyond, skirting its sides.

St Mary's church has an unusual one-handed clock, which is still in working order and is almost certainly Elizabethan. The three church bells were cast at Buckingham between 1590 and 1620.

The elegant red brick house alongside the church was the rectory, designed in 1832 by the renowned architect, Gilbert Scott. Scott also designed the village school, two houses and a granary and a cart hovel in the farmyard of Rectory Farm.

Life in Wappenham has gone on quietly for centuries, with just the odd moment of excitement! Despite his connections with the church, a certain Mr Theophilus Hart, who came into the village in 1642, was renowned for his extra-marital activities with the butcher's wife. The butcher was, to say the least, not amused. One day in 1686 – after a long chase over fields and hedges – the butcher caught and murdered Theophilus. At the time, the ardent lover was aged at least 65!

⌘ WARMINGTON

The first documentary evidence of the existence of Warmington came in a charter of AD 660. The village grew substantially during relatively prosperous times for agriculture, and the wealth generated led to the building of the present church being started in the 12th century. The church, dedicated to Mary the Virgin, is notable among county churches for its vaulted roof. Over the ensuing centuries there have been various additions to it.

The village continued to thrive until the greater agricultural depression began around 1874 when there was much desertion of the land, several bankruptcies among farmers, and the village population began to decline. This decline was not really halted until the First World War when the government dictated what crops were to be grown.

Since the Second World War, in common with other villages, the scene has become less agricultural and Warmington is now more of a dormitory village for Peterborough. The mill is no longer a working one. There is no longer a shoemaker, blacksmith, wheelwright, baker, tailor or carrier. Community spirit remains, however, kept alive by the various clubs and societies in the village.

Across the road is Eaglethorpe (once a village itself) and the river Nene. There is an old mill and many boats moor here. There are walks across the locks and for the energetic a footpath to Fotheringhay.

Warmington Mill

⌘ WEEDON-BEC

Weedon-Bec, a village steeped in history, lies close to the Roman Watling Street, which crosses the river Nene in the region of the church of St Peter and St Paul. Weedon-Bec derives its name from its connections with the abbey of Bec Hellonin, dating from the 12th century, in France.

The village of today appears to be split into three sections. There is the old village with its thatched cottages, brick terraces and Northamptonshire stone walls; Upper Weedon, with views of the historic Royal Military Depot; and Road Weedon.

St Peter's church nestles between the Grand Union Canal and the railway line. To the south of this site, a chapel once stood dedicated to St Werburgh. This area of land was known as Ashyards and at different times over the ages, large stones have been retrieved from here, in all probability being ruins of St Werburgh's Priory. St Werburgh is best remembered for the persuasive way in which she banished a flock of wild geese which were plaguing the cornfields of Weedon. The geese obeyed her and have never been seen over Weedon from that time!

One of Weedon's most familiar buildings must be the old school, which when it was founded and endowed in 1712 was known as the Free School. A native of Weedon, by the name of Nathaniel Billing, after the death of his wife, converted all his personal estate into money to provide 20 poor children of the village with the chance to be educated.

Alice Old was one of Weedon's oldest residents. Inscribed on her gravestone, which lies to the south of St Peter's church, is a list of six sovereigns throughout whose reigns she had lived, commencing with Elizabeth I and ending with William and Mary.

The Royal Military Depot was established here in 1803, when it was considered that as Weedon was situated in the heart of England, it would be a safe place for King George III and other members of the Royal Family to come to in the event of a French invasion. Also troops could be easily sent from her to any part of England. The barracks became redundant in 1965.

⌘ WELFORD

Even before the Domesday Book was produced in 1086, Welford was established. By 1274 there was a weekly Friday market, and the annual fair was held on the Feast of the Annunciation of the Blessed Virgin Mary, August 15th, and the two following days.

The church was once a chapel of ease of the nearby Sulby Abbey and the underground tunnel which supposedly joined the two is marked by strange 'echoing' sounds across the fields in its path. In 1968 great excitement was aroused when two brothers, Jack and Jim Vaughan, digging holes for posts for new fencing in a farmer's field, unearthed a small black object. They threw it on one side, but eventually took it home, cleaned it up and realised it was a piece of Church plate. Subsequently it was presented before a court who decided it was a 15th century chalice and declared it Treasure Trove. It is now in the British Museum and is known as the Welford Chalice.

In the stagecoach days, Welford (being halfway between Leicester and Northampton) emerged as an important resting place, there being seven inns or coaching houses along the length of the present High Street. The canal and the railway both played their part in the development of the village, and the canal is now a popular leisure facility, with boats for hire at the end of the Welford Arm.

⌘ WELTON

Welton is a charming residential hilltop village on the western edge of the county, close to the Warwickshire border. Its name is derived from the springs and wells in the locality.

The church, dedicated to St Martin, is situated up the steep winding hill, sheltered by the still rising hill to the west and north. Inside, the building is light and airy. The ancient tub-shaped font, reputed to be Saxon, is said to have been dragged from East Anglia in one piece. In 1899, inspired by the saintly Canon Lidel, five villagers carved the beautiful pulpit and the alms box, representing an open hand.

In the churchyard most of the gravestones have been thrown down and are now grassed over, soon to be lost for ever. One still standing marks the grave of a six year old boy found starved to death in 1806: its touching little verse at the base has now crumbled.

Welton Place was built in the 18th century, on a site selected by Joseph Clarke and his brother Richard. In the 19th century rare trees were planted on the hill behind the house and round the magnificent lake. Some of the cedars are still there, with the preservation order on them. The little garden flower clarkia is accredited to the Clarke family.

The estate was surrounded by lovely stone walls, some still standing – one with an archway leading to the church opposite. Welton Place was in the Clarke family for well over a century and was known to villagers as 'The Big House' and, of course, the head of the Clarke family was the squire of the village.

The mansion was let to Major and Mrs Garrard, who were the Crown Jewellers, and the family was often visited by members of the Royal Family. Later the building was converted into flats but subsequently demolished.

⌘ WHILTON & WHILTON LOCKS

The church clock at Whilton is Elizabethan and is peculiar in that the dial has only

A narrowboat glides by at Whilton Locks

four minutes marked to each five minute interval. As this dial has not been altered since first installed it may indicate that the inhabitants of Whilton have always been able to tolerate a little wayward behaviour!

This tolerance may have been rather strained, however, by the terms of the will of one of their more eccentric rectors – Langton Freeman. In his will of 1783 he gave the following instructions. 'For four or five days after my decease and till my body grows offensive I would not be removed out of the place or bed I shall die on and then I would be carried and laid on the same bed decently and privately in the summerhouse in the garden . . . and to be wrapped in a strong double winding sheet and . . . to be interred as near as may be to the description we receive of our Saviour's burial. The door and windows to be locked . . . the summerhouse be planted round with evergreen plants and fenced with iron or oak panels and painted dark blue.' The summerhouse has disappeared and no one knows what later became of the Rev Langton Freeman. Perhaps his spirit still haunts the garden of what is now known as the Manor House.

Whilton has a long history of adapting to change resulting from its geographical position. Almost the centre of the country, it has two Roman roads passing through the parish and gained its first importance as a Roman settlement and staging post on the Watling Street running from London to Holyhead. This road remains a major trunk road but now there is the M1 running parallel, and with its more modern service area adjacent. The Grand Union Canal, constructed in the 1780s, also runs parallel as does the London to Birmingham railway built in the 1860s.

Nowadays, although all trace of the original manor has been lost, Whilton still possesses a number of pleasant older houses, a cob cottage and a picturesque church. The mill ceased to function in living memory. One of the smaller stone houses of 1689 is said to contain floorboards made from the doors of the old prison in Northampton. It was sold in the Depression in 1932 for a sow and a litter of pigs! Practically all the older houses seem at one time or another to have served as shops, or tradesmen's dwellings. In 1777 the main occupations related to the wool trade – wool combing, spinning, weaving and framework knitting, and shoemaking. In the 19th and early 20th century it was almost a self-contained community with butcher, slaughterhouse, bakehouse, alehouses, wheelwrights, blacksmith, carpenter and undertakers, carriers, dressmakers and lacemaker, not to mention the school.

The school began in 1768 in a farm and buildings left by Jonathan Emery an ancestor of a family still farming in the village. Five hundred pounds and 11 acres of land went with the bequest and a later benefactor, Mrs John Worsfold, in 1815 gave money which purchased 15 acres of land: 'to instruct the poor children of the parish in reading, writing, casting of accounts, the church catechism and the principles of the Christian religion'. These wills seem a distinct improvement on that of Langton Freeman. The schoolhouse has now reverted to being a private dwelling but the schoolroom has become the village hall and some at least of its original intentions continue.

The thriving community of Whilton Locks gains its name from the flight of locks on the Grand Union Canal. In days gone by Whilton Locks boasted a pub, the Spotted Cow, a blacksmith, a grocery and lime kilns. One bargee, John Woodward, used to keep donkeys as well as horses to pull barges. Apparently, he never swore and was known as 'the beautiful man and his donkeys'.

But by far Whilton Locks' best claim to fame is that it is thought to be the site of the birthplace of St Patrick of Ireland. During the Roman occupation, in the fields where Whilton Lodge now stands, was once a Roman settlement, known as 'Bannaventa' and it is here that the infant Patrick is said to have been born, subsequently going to Cornwall and then to Ireland. Excavations have revealed Samian ware and coins at Bannaventa but unfortunately the site has now been ploughed.

⌘ WHITTLEBURY

Four miles from Towcester and seven miles from Buckingham stands Whittlebury, on the A413. Travelling from Silverstone, Whittlebury is seen to dominate the ridge of a hill. It is a small village steeped in history.

Several Iron Age and Roman sites lay within part of Whittlewood Forest, which skirted the village. Following her last battle against the Romans, Queen Boadicea is reputed to have been buried in the forest.

Much to his surprise one villager, enlarging his garden path, came across a shallow grave containing a Roman skeleton. As it was obvious that a Christian burial had taken place, the Rev Peter Townsend, in May 1983, reburied the remains in St Mary's churchyard.

Excavations in a stone-pit in 1850 discovered the remains of buildings. One contained at least twelve rooms and a bath suite. The mosaic pavement was a striking design of red and white. The second building lay to the north of the site and had two mosaic floors.

Stag's Head House, built in 1834, is situated on the corner of High Street and Church Way; a house once loved by housewives, for this was the bakery. On Sunday these ladies would take their joints of beef etc there to be roasted, whilst they went to church. Imagine the aroma at that corner!

John Wesley preached on 20 occasions at Whittlebury Methodist chapel. According to his journal he first spoke 'To a truly loving and simple people. I preached at the side of the new preaching house. I suppose most of the town were present.' The pulpit is still the one he used.

⌘ WILBARSTON

The village was once part of the Rockingham estate and is surrounded by farmland, truly green and pleasant. It nestles in the picturesque Welland valley in an area formerly covered by Rockingham Forest.

The 12th century church of All Saints is worthy of a visit to see the unusual painted ceiling and beautifully carved oak screen. Close by is the 17th century Old House, where the ghosts of Sir George and a nun are reputed to have appeared after the removal of certain gravestones. Since the Bishop of Peterborough used the house as a robing room in 1973, the ghosts have not been seen!

Another interesting feature is the number of springs under the village keeping the many wells constantly supplied. These were in use up to the introduction of piped water in 1957. Some pumps and wells are still operational.

Wilbarston has always been a caring village. Indeed in 1791 Robert Swan gave 11s a year to the poor and 3s 4d for an annual sermon. This was later known as 'Swan's Charity', with £2 being donated for the purchase of 'red flannel', given alternate years to elderly ladies and gentlemen of the parish. Later, every four years, elderly residents were chosen to receive a pair of towels. Today, existing charities have been amalgamated to form Wilbarston Relief in Need Charity.

The modern community hall caused comment in *Punch* when the winning entry in the 'Name the village hall' competition, provided the name 'The Village Hall'!

⌘ WOLLASTON

When Wollaston first developed it grew along a 'line'. This started at Cobbs Lane and continued past the 'clusters' of Bell End at one end and Rotten Row/St Michael's Lane at the other end of the High Street, and continued towards Strixton. The name of Wollaston comes from Wulflaf's Town, Wulflaf being an early Saxon.

The oldest part of the village is Beacon Hill, which is an ancient castle earthwork which belonged to Bury Manor, and which used to be called Mill Hill. It was surrounded by a great ditch which, when investigated, was found to date back to the 12th century.

The lovely mottled red/orange bricks around Wollaston no doubt came from the two brickyards in Wollaston itself (one along the Grendon Road, near Cringle Farm, and the other where the industrial estate now exists). If you look closely, you can see that the patterns of the courses are different from the way houses are built today; some have a chequerboard effect, some look striped. Another interesting feature is the way bricks are laid according to the lie of the land; if the land sloped, the wall sloped too. This is particularly noticeable when walls have been recently repaired. The repair will be level whilst the rest of the wall will be at an angle.

The High Street was at one time cobbled and this is sometimes visible when the road starts to wear at the edge. The smithy (or forge) was located opposite the Methodist church and part of it can still be seen.

⌘ WOODFORD

Woodford's lovely church of St Mary the Virgin stands majestically by the river Nene. Inserted in one of the pillars on the north side of the nave is a glass case containing the remains of a human heart, found during restoration work to the column in 1867. There are many theories about whose heart it is and one story is that it belonged to a gallant knight killed on the Crusades, whose heart was returned to the village by his friends. It was possibly the heart of one of the Traillys, lord of the manor 700 years ago.

Like all small villages at the turn of the century Woodford was self-sufficient in trade and industry. One of the major industries was mining. There was ironstone mining, also limestone pits and furnaces. All of these industries employed a number of men from Woodford, Twywell, Slipton and Islip. The work was hard, but there were happenings on the lighter side. One of these was the way the men earned a little extra cash. Horses were used down the pits and the men grew mushrooms on the manure. Twice a week the mushrooms were taken to Covent Garden and sold. The money was then divided between the men.

Later in the 1930s and 1940s Woodford had two bakehouses and two fish and chip shops, one of which had a bad fire when the pans set on fire. There

Across the fields to Woodford village

was also an undertaker who made coffins in the shed in the yard of his house. Cobbling was also a busy trade. One or two people mended shoes in their own homes, but Mr Cyril Wilson had a shop on the green where he not only mended shoes but made them as well, including boots for the men working in the furnaces.

⌘ YARDLEY GOBION

The village of Yardley Gobion lies near the southern tip of the county of Northamptonshire; to the east it is flanked by the Grand Union Canal and the river Tove whilst to the west there are open fields to the A5.

Until 1947 the village was virtually only the High Street, Moor End Road, Chestnut Road and Grafton Road, with a sympathetic mixture of stone or brick, thatched or slated houses. The council estate (built in 1947) was followed by two private estates in the late 1960s which, with the limited infill development since then, has expanded the village.

The Anglican church, St Leonard's, is relatively modern, having been built in 1864 by the Duke of Grafton, who added a clock over the porch in 1889. However, a church dedicated to St Leonard existed in former times on the site of what is now 1 High Street, with the churchyard on the land adjoining the High Street/Grafton Road bend. Between times and for those who eschewed High Church, a United Reformed chapel was built in 1826 overlooking Chestnut

Green; regular services are still held. Within St Leonard's there is a lectern dedicated to eight Canadian airmen whose aircraft crashed on the outskirts of the village (between the High Street and the new bypass) in 1944.

When Orchard Close (a small housing development off the High Street) was being built in 1968, post-medieval pottery kilns were found on the site, together with large quantities of 18th century slate. Further finds of kilns show that from the 14th century Yardley Gobion had a substantial pottery industry.

On the outskirts but forming part of the village is Moor End, first mentioned in 1304. In 1347, Thomas de Ferrers was given licence by Edward III to build a castle, tower, moat and bridge. However, in 1363 the land reverted to the Crown before the castle was completed in 1369. The castle (and its manor) were last recorded in 1541 although the site is still marked on OS maps and Moor End Manor Farm still flourishes. During the Civil War, Moor End was taken from the Crown by the Parliamentary party but was reclaimed by the Crown during the Restoration of Charles II. In turn, Charles II gave it to his son, the 1st Duke of Grafton, and it remained with his heirs until the breakup of the Grafton Estate in 1919–1920.

Just within the parish of Yardley Gobion (beyond Moor End) is the famous Queen's Oak; here, Elizabeth Woodville (or Wideville as it was then spelt) first met King Edward IV whom she later married on 1st May 1464 at Grafton Regis, about one and a half miles north of Yardley Gobion. Their children were the ill-fated 'Princes in the Tower'.

⌘ YELVERTOFT

Yelvertoft is not a conventionally pretty village, but the cottages which line the main street have a charm of their own. Some of them are right on the pavement, others stand back, while 19th century cottages butt up against Georgian farmhouses. The four main lanes run at right angles to the main street, and their names are reminders of long-past farmers – Ward's, Tarry's, Swinnerton's and Ashwell's.

Life in the 1920s and 1930s seems in retrospect so much more peaceful. In the early years of the century the wharf on the Grand Union Canal was still busy and the horse and trap remained the only means of land transport for a long time after that. There were two bakers, a blacksmith, a grocer, a butcher and three inns. A traveller would come from Northampton with other items and it was also possible to order goods through the carrier from Rugby. In 1887 the village celebrated Queen Victoria's Golden Jubilee. When all the bills were paid for the day of revelry and sports, enough money was left over to buy three lime trees. Rev Jenkins planted one on the green in the centre of the village, Rev Parkins of the Congregational church planted one on the green opposite the reading room, and Mr Elkins, a local gentleman, planted one beside the school. They stand today as links with the villagers of the past.